A Little Book of Latin Love Poetry

Teacher's Guide

by

JOHN BREUKER and MARDAH B. C. WEINFIELD

Bolchazy-Carducci Publishers, Inc.
Wauconda, Illinois USA

General Editors:
Marie Carducci Bolchazy
Laurie Haight Keenan

Cover Illustration:
Wallpainting of Young girl, from Pompeii, Italy. Style of the 4th century BCE.
Museo Archeologico Nazionale, Naples, Italy. Erich Lessing / Art Resource, NY.

Cover Design & Typography:
Adam Phillip Velez

**A Little Book of Latin Love Poetry
Teacher's Guide**

John Breuker & Mardah B. C. Weinfield

© 2007 Bolchazy-Carducci Publishers, Inc.
All rights reserved

Bolchazy-Carducci Publishers, Inc.
1000 Brown Street, Unit 101
Wauconda, Illinois 60084
www.bolchazy.com

Printed in the United States of America
2007
by Publisher's Graphics

ISBN 978-0-86516-636-3

CONTENTS

Introduction v

Standards for Classical Language Learning vii

Preface (from Student Text) ix

Notes to Students (from Student Text) xi

Answer Key: Selections I–XI 1

Unit Review Answer Key 63

Sample "Alternative Assessment Projects" 123

Bibliography 155

INTRODUCTION TO THE TEACHER'S GUIDE

The *Teacher's Guide* contains a wide variety of information with which each teacher may customize his/her presentations for the students. We have reprinted each modified selection in large font and provided a literal translation for each. Sample answers are given for all questions posed in the Reading Helps or in the sections entitled Analysis and Comprehension of the Latin Text as well as for all the exercises in the Rapid Reviews and the Major Reviews. We have also given possible responses for the Questions of Literary Analysis and Discussion. The Unit Review contains a clean copy of the unmodified text of each Latin poem as well as a literal translation of each. For those teachers who choose to introduce and/or discuss metrics, we have provided a scanned copy of each unmodified poem. Lastly, we have supplied possible responses to the Points to Ponder, although these questions tend to be more open-ended and subjective in nature.

As we stated in the Preface to *A Little Book of Latin Love Poetry* (hereafter *Libellus*), we have tried to incorporate standards-based learning and assessment wherever possible:

> The *Libellus* addresses in a very direct manner Goals 1, 3 and 5 in their entirety. If one considers a poem a "product" of the Romans, then Goal 2.2 is also addressed directly. Goals 2.1 and 4.2 are approached indirectly in the Introductions to the authors and lend themselves to projects outside of class at the discretion and wish of the teacher. Goal 4.1 in also approached indirectly throughout the *Libellus*, and directly in several Rapid Reviews, some FYIs (e.g. p. 77), and in the Major Reviews. [For a listing of the Standards for Classical Learning, see next page.]

The *Teacher's Guide* also contains sample projects relating the historical period, people, and poetry, which teachers may modify for their own use. Additional stimulating ideas are available in the works cited in the bibliographical section. While by no means intended to be a complete bibliography, we did want to alert teachers to those works we have consulted most frequently, both for our own day-to-day teaching and in preparation for this book.

John Breuker, Jr.
Mardah B. C. Weinfield

A Note about Selection X-A & B, Ovid *Amores* I.5

During field testing of the *Libellus*, some teachers expressed discomfort with the specificity of four lines in Ovid *Amores*, I.5: lines 19–22. Therefore, the *Libellus* omits these lines. For teachers who <u>are</u> comfortable with the content of these lines, we have provided unexpurgated versions on pages 53–54 and 111 in the Teacher's Guide. We have also provided necessary Reading Helps, Vocabulary, Discussion and Review Materials for these four lines.

J.B. and M.B.C.W.

STANDARDS FOR CLASSICAL LANGUAGE LEARNING*

Goal 1: COMMUNICATION
Communicate in a Classical Language

- Standard 1.1 Students read, understand, and interpret Latin or Greek.
- Standard 1.2 Students use orally, listen to, and write Latin or Greek as part of the language learning process.

Goal 2: CULTURE
Gain Knowledge and Understanding of Greco-Roman Culture

- Standard 2.1 Students demonstrate an understanding of the perspectives of Greek or Roman culture as revealed in the practices of the Greeks or Romans.
- Standard 2.2 Students demonstrate an understanding of the perspectives of Greek or Roman culture as revealed in the products of the Greeks or Romans.

Goal 3: CONNECTIONS
Connect with Other Disciplines and Expand Knowledge

- Standard 3.1 Students reinforce and further their knowledge of other disciplines through their study of classical languages.
- Standard 3.2 Students expand their knowledge through the reading of Latin or Greek and the study of ancient culture.

Goal 4: COMPARISONS
Develop Insight into Own Language and Culture

- Standard 4.1 Students recognize and use elements of the Latin or Greek language to increase knowledge of their own language.
- Standard 4.2 Students compare and contrast their own culture with that of the Greco-Roman world.

Goal 5: COMMUNITIES
Participate in Wider Communities of Language and Culture

- Standard 5.1 Students use their knowledge of Latin or Greek in a multilingual world.
- Standard 5.2 Students use their knowledge of Greco-Roman culture in a world of diverse cultures.

---

* Reproduced with permission from "Standards for Classical Language Learning," ACL, Oxford, Ohio, 1997.

PREFACE (FROM THE STUDENT TEXT)

Our goal in writing the *Libellus* is to introduce students, generally at the third/fourth semester high school level or the late second/early third semester college level, to mainstream Latin poets and to ease their transition to reading these authors. To this end, our reader contains passages of both modified and authentic Latin verse. We have modified carefully selected Latin passages in order to make them more accessible to beginning readers (see paragraph 4). When combined with the extensive vocabulary and reading support provided, the modified passages provide a bridge from syntax, grammar, vocabulary and individual sentences (the elements of reading) to the coherent whole of connected authentic Latin literature (the actuality of reading). The unmodified passages, used as review, contain further annotation and provide familiarity with authentic Latin texts and meters. These unmodified passages enable the teacher and student to address literary, metrical, humanistic, philological and comprehension concerns beyond those already introduced in connection with the modified texts. As much as possible, we have attempted to align the content and presentation of material with the Standards for Classical Language Learning.

The *Libellus* addresses in a very direct manner Goals 1, 3 and 5 in their entirety. If one considers a poem a "product" of the Romans, then Goal 2.2 is also addressed directly. Goals 2.1 and 4.2 are approached indirectly in the Introductions to the authors and lend themselves to projects outside of class at the discretion and wish of the teacher. Goal 4.1 in also approached indirectly throughout the *Libellus*, and directly in several Rapid Reviews, some FYIs (e.g. p. 77), and in the Major Reviews.

The Latin passages focus on a theme prevalent in the Roman world and our own: Love. We chose this theme to capture the interest of students and because it resonates throughout the works of Rome's major authors. The authors included—Catullus, Horace and Ovid—were selected because in most curricula they are among the first to be read following the acquisition of fundamental vocabulary and the syntactical/grammatical bases essential to reading.

We have chosen to modify the Latin Passages because, in our experience, students new to reading authentic Latin literature are often overwhelmed by the multiple tasks they must perform simultaneously. When reading, students must deal with issues of vocabulary, syntax/grammar, unfamiliar forms, word order, and—in poetry—meter and figures of speech. This *Libellus* addresses these issues in the following ways:

1) Extensive reading vocabulary accompanies each passage, together with a full glossary in the back of the book. A few unusual words have been replaced with more common ones.

2) Reading Helps address issues of syntax/grammar and form. Rapid Reviews address syntax/grammar which many students find problematical.

3) Modified Latin delays issues of poetic word order and metrical considerations until the unit review.

4) Poetic devices are included and defined, where appropriate, <u>throughout</u> the *Libellus*.

It is our intent that this transitional reader will fuse components of both the inductive and deductive methodologies that permeate the classrooms of the twenty-first century, and that it will be of particular use in standards-based learning and assessment. We also believe that this volume will make starting to read Latin literature more pleasurable and less onerous for students, thus increasing their appreciation of Rome's contributions to our literary and humanistic heritage.

We gratefully acknowledge significant encouragement received during this endeavor. Lou and Marie Bolchazy from Bolchazy-Carducci Publishers initiated the project and shepherded it at each stage to its conclusion. Our editor, Laurie Haight Keenan, provided countless incisive suggestions and an eagle eye for detail. The Trustees of Western Reserve Academy and its Headmaster, Dr. Henry E. Flanagan, awarded a sabbatical leave and generously provided an additional academic year released from classroom obligations to enable continued writing. Congenial colleagues around the country cooperated in field-testing preliminary drafts; without their generous spirit and suggestions for improvement a far less effective version would have resulted. Any remaining infelicities or errors are our responsibility. Finally, and most of all, our spouses have been understanding, supportive and patient to a degree far beyond the norm. To one and all we address the words of appreciation spoken by Trojan Aeneas to Queen Dido for the Carthaginians' warm welcome to his storm-tossed voyagers:

> *grātēs persolvere dignās/nōn opis est nostrae.*
> To offer deserved thanks is not within our power.
> Vergil, *Aeneid* I.600–601

JOHN BREUKER, JR.
MARDAH B. C. WEINFIELD

NOTES TO STUDENTS (FROM THE STUDENT TEXT)

We have organized this *Libellus* to provide students with maximum support as they begin the process of reading and interpreting authentic Latin texts. For unmodified Latin text, we have selected the Loeb versions, and it is from these that we then created the modified Latin versions.

We have altered the authentic text in four ways. First, we have rearranged the word order into more easily recognized thought units ("chunks"). Second, we have simplified some vocabulary, grammatical forms and constructions, as needed. Third, we have sometimes omitted one or more lines of difficult authentic text. Finally, we have at times changed punctuation or spelling. Because of these changes, the modified versions lose some of their metrical quality (i.e. they do not completely scan). The unmodified text for each selection appears in the Unit Review, where a Textual Matters section highlights significant differences between the modified and unmodified texts. This is an appropriate time to consider meter and scansion. A brief discussion of metrics is found in **Appendix C**.

We introduce each author with a concise biography and, in addition, we briefly summarize and describe in context each Latin selection. Regarding the authors, we recognize that each writer may be understood in two ways—as he really was and as his literary *persōna* (his mask) indicates. We devote a section of each biography to a description of that author's *persōna*, but for the sake of clarity we have chosen to minimize our presentation of this topic in the selection summaries.

To aid in the reading of each Latin selection, students will find extensive Vocabulary and Reading Helps on each left-hand page, designed to address issues associated with the Latin text which stands opposite on the right-hand page. In the Reading Helps, we have at times deliberately posed questions. We did so for two reasons: 1) to help the students decipher important clues for understanding the text, and 2) to show the students the kind of mental questions they should be asking themselves as they read a Latin passage. With each question, we try to make its answer apparent. For any vocabulary words not listed opposite the Latin text, a full glossary/dictionary is located at the back of the volume.

Under each modified selection is a list of questions, which we have created to aid in the understanding and interpretation of the selection's text. We have included questions of two types: 1) Analysis and Comprehension of the Latin Text, and 2) Literary Analysis and Discussion.

1. Questions analyzing the Latin text are those which ask about matters of vocabulary and/or syntax so that the student will be able to read/translate the Latin text accurately: Is the *ut* clause indicating purpose or result? Does the *cum* indicate manner or accompaniment? How can one decide if *vēnī* is a singular, present imperative form of *veniō* or a 1st person, singular, perfect, active, indicative form of the verb? Comprehension questions are those which, based upon accurate textual analysis, check on the reader's understanding of a passage's meaning/content: What is the antecedent of this pronoun? How many characters appear in this poem? What four physical characteristics does the passage give for character A?

2. Literary Analysis and Discussion: questions, based upon accurate analysis and comprehension of the Latin text, which deal with the passage as literature to be interpreted, suggest topics for discussion in the classroom or for interpretation in a short essay, or ask the student's opinion based upon his/her understanding of the passage: What impact does the sight of A have upon B? What is ambiguous about the poet's word choice of _____? How does the poet's use of a poetic figure (e.g. onomatopoeia) enhance the passage's literary quality? Why, based upon your reading of the passage, do you think the poet does this, but not that?

There are also questions in the Unit Review, where the student will find Points to Ponder for each unmodified selection. These questions generally are more open-ended and broader in nature, designed to help the student draw connections among the various selections, and among the authors as well.

Following each modified selection is a Rapid Review of a particular grammatical or syntactical topic associated with that selection. The information contained in the Rapid Reviews is based upon the grammars of Gildersleeve and Bennett, and the dictionary of Traupman, all of which are available in paperbook editions from Bolchazy-Carducci Publishers. Our expectation is that a teacher choosing to use this book will have these references available for students' use. This *Libellus*, however, does contain an Appendix (**Appendix D**) of essential forms, syntax and grammar.

We recognize that not *all* the review material will necessarily have been studied by *all* students, but the reviews *have* been designed to include material covered by *most* high school students at the end of the third semester, and by *most* college students at the end of the second semester. Since our book strives to ease the transition from a basic textbook to reading authentic authors for students from a wide background of methodologies, we wish to emphasize that we expect the students using our books to have a comfortable grasp of the topics of grammar, morphology and syntax recommended to be covered by these semester/year benchmarks in the latest professional discussions of standards. (Chapter 11 in S. Davis, *Latin in American Schools. Teaching the Ancient World*. Atlanta, 1991, especially pp. 54–58, and Chapter 5: "National Standards and Curriculum Guidelines" by M. G. Abbott, S. Davis and R. C. Gascoyne in R. A. LaFleur (ed), *Latin for the 21st Century. From Concept to Classroom*. Glenville, IL, 1998, especially pp. 52–56. See the Addendum on the following page for a sample listing of the syntax topics.)

We also recognize that many of the topics which these lists specify are so thoroughly familiar to almost all students as to need no review. We have chosen as Rapid Review (RR) topics, therefore, those which our own teaching experiences have shown to be problematic for many students. Generally speaking, these topics are covered in the second high school year or second college semester. The following topics are reviewed in this *Libellus*, as they are met in the context of a selected passage:

RR 1: temporal clauses
RR 2: vocatives and imperatives
RR 3: correlative pairings
RR 4: formation of the present tense of the subjunctive mood
RR 5: five uses of the tricky word *quam*
RR 6: interrogative pronouns and adjectives
RR 7: enclitics
RR 8: comparison of adjectives
RR 9: conditional sentences
RR 10: deponent verbs
RR 11: irregular verbs
RR 12: the formation and comparison of adverbs
RR 13: demonstrative adjectives/pronouns

Each Rapid Review includes practice exercises on its topic and, in addition, the *Libellus* contains two Major Reviews, one of infinitive forms and usages, and one of participle forms and usages. Each Major Review includes multiple exercises for practice with each substantive section of the review. We have chosen not to emphasize a review of subjunctive forms and usages because there are relatively few to be found in the passages which appear in this volume.

ANSWER KEY: SELECTIONS I–XI

SELECTION I

TRANSLATION

      That man (He) to me seems to be equal to a god,
      That man (he), if it is right (to say so), to me seems to surpass the gods,
      Who, sitting opposite you, again and again looks at you
      And hears you laughing sweetly
5   (A thing) which snatches away all senses for (from) wretched me:

      For as soon as I (have) beheld you, Lesbia,
      No voice is left over in my mouth
      But my tongue is numb,
      A thin flame spreads down beneath my joints,
10   My ears ring with their own sound,
      And my eyes are covered by twin night (darkness).

READING HELPS

Line 11 *geminā nocte* suggests "twin/double darkness." The string of physical effects occasioned by the sight of Lesbia culminates in a swoon/fainting spell.

SELECTION I

    Ille mī pār esse deō vidētur,
    ille, sī fās est, mī superāre dīvōs vidētur,
    quī sedēns adversus identidem tē spectat
    et tē dulce rīdentem audit,
5   quod omnēs sensūs mihi miserō ēripit:

    nam simul atque tē, Lesbia, aspexī,
    nihil vōcis mī in ōre superest
    sed lingua torpet,
    tenuis flamma sub artūs dēmānat,
10 aurēs sonitū suō tintinnant,
    et lūmina mea geminā nocte teguntur.

ANALYSIS AND COMPREHENSION OF THE LATIN TEXT

1. *Ille* refers to the scenario's man who is sitting with Lesbia, *mī/mihi* refers to the poet and *tē* refers to Lesbia.
2. The antecedent of *quī* is *Ille,* and the (understood) antecedent of *quod* is *id,* referring to the situation described in the *quī . . . audit* clauses.

LITERARY ANALYSIS AND DISCUSSION

1. Lines 5–11 in the text suggest the impact of seeing Lesbia on the poet. Line 5 provides a <u>general statement</u> of introduction—the person opposite her looks at her and listens to her but the poet is *miser* for he loses *omnēs* his *sensūs*. Lines 6–11 provide a <u>detailed listing</u> of the impact on his *sensūs*: as soon as he has seen Lesbia, he loses his voice (line 7), his tongue is numb (line 8), he feels warm (line 9), his ears ring (line 10), and he swoons (line 11).

    The description is generally considered **HYPERBOLE,** an attempt to flatter the lovely woman.

RAPID REVIEW #1

1. After I (had) beheld you, no voice remained in my mouth.
2. When that man (had) sat facing you, all senses were snatched away from wretched me.
3. As soon as I (had) heard you laughing sweetly, Lesbia, my tongue was numb.
4. Before my eyes are covered by twin night, a thin flame spreads down beneath my joints.
5. While my tongue is numb, my ears ring with their (own) sound.
6. When our brief light has set, one eternal night must be slept.
7. While (As long as) I was pleasing to you, I was more blessed than the king of the Persians.
8. The sun comes back when night has gone away.
9. As/When the girl (had) stood before my eyes, I saw no flaw in/on her body.
10. When we (will) have made many thousand kisses (thousands of kisses), we'll mix them up.

SELECTION II

TRANSLATION

    Hello, girl, with neither a very small nose
    Nor a pretty foot nor dark eyes
    Nor long fingers nor a dry mouth
    Nor, to be sure, too elegant a tongue.
5   You the province says to be pretty?
    With you our (my) Lesbia is compared?
    Oh, a tasteless and witless (clueless) generation!

READING HELPS

Line 3   *Salvē* is a singular imperative.

Line 5   No form of the verb *teneō* has the initial cluster *tēn-*. The verb's singular imperative is *tenē*.

SELECTION II

> Salvē, puella, nec minimō nāsō
> nec bellō pede nec nigrīs ocellīs
> nec longīs digitīs nec ōre siccō
> nec sānē nimis ēlegante linguā.
> 5 Tēne provincia narrat esse bellam?
> Tēcum Lesbia nostra comparātur?
> Ō saeculum insapiēns et infacētum!

ANALYSIS AND COMPREHENSION OF THE LATIN TEXT

1. The six features the girl does not possess are: a very small nose, a pretty foot, dark eyes, long fingers, a dry mouth nor an elegant tongue.
2. The characters in the poem are the *puella*, the people in the *provincia*, Lesbia, and the people included in the *nostra* (either Catullus and his friends or, if *nostra* equals *mea*, Catullus himself).

LITERARY ANALYSIS AND DISCUSSION

1. A colloquial tone and light-hearted mood may be established by the poet's use of the informal *salvē*.
2. An effect of the **ANAPHORA** of *nec* is a strong emphasis on all the features the girl does NOT possess. The negative word may be emphasized to add emotional intensity and, perhaps, to highlight the implicit suggestion that Lesbia by contrast DOES have these features.
3. The poet may choose to name Lesbia but not the girl because the real point of the poem may be praise for Lesbia's urbane beauty rather than censure of the provincial *puella*'s ordinariness or unattractiveness.
4. The ambiguity lies in the possibility that *nostra* can be taken to mean "our" or "my." If "our," the poet shares Lesbia with someone (her husband? another lover? his friends into whose fellowship she has entered?); if "my," it's an example of the commonly seen poetic plural/editorial plural/royal "we."
5. The **ANAPHORA** of *tē* in lines 5–6 highlights the poet's apparent disbelief. He seems to find it incredible that "YOU" (i.e. the *puella*) are compared to Lesbia.
6. The *puella* lacks the features which Lesbia possesses. What the *puella* does NOT have, Lesbia by implication does.

RAPID REVIEW #2
PRACTICE A

1.	agricola	agricolae	6.	mīles	mīlitēs
2.	cīvis	cīvēs	7.	Publī	Publiī
3.	fīlia	fīliae	8.	rex	rēgēs
4.	fīlī	fīliī	9.	Rōmāne	Rōmānī
5.	imperātor	imperātōrēs	10.	mī serve	meī servī

PRACTICE B

1.	amā	amāte	6.	fer	ferte
2.	cape	capite	7.	nōlī	nōlīte
3.	dīc	dīcite	8.	pōne	pōnite
4.	dūc	dūcite	9.	terrē	terrēte
5.	fac	facite	10.	venī	venīte

PRACTICE C

	Vocatives	Imperatives
1.	Lesbia	
2.	puella	salvē
3.	mea Lesbia	
4.	puella . . . Scelesta	Valē
5.	Catulle	obdūrā
6.	Chloē	
7.	dīva . . . regīna	tange
8.		dēsine
9.	Catulle	
10.		Da
11.	Miser Catulle	
12.		pōnite
13.	Attice	crēde
14.		frangite

SELECTION III

TRANSLATION

    Quintia is beautiful to many;
    To me she is fair-skinned, tall, and has a good posture:
    I grant these things thus (in such a way) one-by-one.
    I deny that totality to be beautiful (that that totality is beautiful): for there is not any charm,
5   Not any taste (wit) in so large (great) a body.
    Lesbia is beautiful, who both is very pretty as a whole
    And alone (all by herself) has stolen (taken away) all the "Venuses" (qualities of the Venuses) from all (women).

SELECTION III

> Quintia formōsa est multīs;
> mihi candida, longa, recta est:
> haec ego sīc singula confiteor.
> Tōtum illud esse formōsum negō: nam nulla venustās,
> 5 nulla mīca salis est in tam magnō corpore.
> Lesbia formōsa est, quae et pulcherrima tōta est,
> et omnibus sōla omnēs Venerēs surripuit.

ANALYSIS AND COMPREHENSION OF THE LATIN TEXT

1. The three adjectives in line 2 would normally be connected by conjunctions.
2. The repetition in lines 4–5 is an example of **ANAPHORA**.
3. There are seven qualities of feminine beauty: *formōsa/um* in lines 1, 4, & 6; *candida*; *longa*; *recta*; *venustās/Venerēs*; *mīca salis*; *pulcherrima*. Quintia has the first four, while Lesbia by implication has all seven since she has all the qualities of feminine beauty.

LITERARY ANALYSIS AND DISCUSSION

1. *Singula* means "one by one," or "individual." The adjectives in line 2 are unconnected by the usual conjunctions, and hence illustrate the "one by one" or "individual" nature of *singula*'s meaning.
2. The plurals *omnēs Venerēs* pick up on the plural ideas of *multīs* in line 1 and of *omnibus* in line 7, and they heighten the contrast with line 7's *sōla* ("alone," "all by herself") as well as with the repeated *nulla* ("not any") in lines 4–5. It matters not what qualities of Venus any other "beauty" may possess. Lesbia already embodies all these qualities within herself.

RAPID REVIEW #3
PRACTICE

1. ... nec ... nec ... nec ... nec ... nec ...
2. ... et ... et
3. ... nec ... nec ...
4. ... seu ... seu ...
5. ... et ... et ...
6. ... vel ... vel ...
7. ... et ... et ...
8. ... alter ... alter ...
9. ... ille ... hic ... ; ... hic ... ille ...
10. ... aut ... aut ...

SELECTION IV

TRANSLATION

    Let us live, my Lesbia, and let us love,
    And all the rumors of the too strict old men
    Let us value at an as.
    Suns are able to set and rise again:
5   (but) when the brief light has set once and for all for us,
    one eternal night must be slept (we must sleep).
    Give me a thousand kisses, then a hundred;
    then a second (another) thousand, than a second hundred;
    then all the way to another thousand, then a hundred.
10   Then, since (when) we have made many thousands,
    We'll thoroughly mix them all up, lest we know,
    Or lest any evil man be able to be jealous of (to bewitch) us
    Since he knows that there is so great a number of kisses.

READING HELPS

Line 6   *dormienda* is a future passive participle (cf. FYI below).

SELECTION IV

      Vīvāmus, mea Lesbia, atque amēmus,
      rūmōrēsque omnēs senum sevēriōrum
      ūnīus assis aestimēmus!
      Sōlēs occidere et resurgere possunt:
5   nōbīs cum semel brevis lux occidit,
      nox perpetua ūna dormienda est.
      Da mī bāsia mille, deinde centum;
      deinde mille altera, deinde secunda centum;
      deinde usque altera mille, deinde centum.
10   Deinde, cum mīlia multa fēcerīmus,
      conturbābimus illa, nē sciāmus,
      aut nē quis malus invidēre possit
      cum sciat tantum esse numerum bāsiōrum.

ANALYSIS AND COMPREHENSION OF THE LATIN TEXT

1. The reason given is that life is short and then death is permanent.
2. **METAPHORS** in lines 4–6 include light for life, night and sleeping for death.
3. The two reasons are stated in the two purpose clauses: if the lovers knew how many kisses they had shared they might be embarrassed or recalled to self-control, and if any *malus* became jealous or bewitched them, thus stopping the exchange of kisses.
4. **ALLITERATION**: *s* sounds in line 2, *d* sounds in lines 7–10, *m* sounds in line 10, etc. **ASSONANCE**: *a* sounds in lines 1 and 3. **HYPERBOLE**: valuing <u>all</u> the rumors as <u>one</u> *as*; exchanging 3,300 (!) kisses

LITERARY ANALYSIS AND DISCUSSION

1. The dramatic effect is a triple exhortation or urging for the poet and Lesbia to live and love without regard for what others may say about them and their behavior.
2. *Sōlēs* may be plural and *lux* singular because *lux* is a **METAPHOR** for an individual life, while the *sōlēs* suggest repeated days in a lifetime.

RAPID REVIEW #4
PRACTICE

1. 3rd, sg., pres., pass. indic.
2. 2nd, sg., pres., act. indic.
3. 1st, sg., pres., act. indic.
4. 1st, sg., pres., act. subj.
5. 3rd, pl., pres., act. indic.
6. 3rd, pl., fut., act. indic.
7. 1st, pl., pres., pass. indic.
8. 1st, pl., pres., pass. subj.
9. 2nd, pl., pres., act. subj.
10. 2nd, pl., impf., act. subj.
11. 3rd, sg., pres. indic. (no voice for *fiō*)
12. 3rd, sg., pres. subj.
13. 2nd, pl., pres., act. indic.
14. 2nd, pl., pres., act. subj.
15. 1st, pl., pres., act. indic.
16. 1st, pl., pres., act. subj.
17. 1st, pl., pf., act. indic.
18. 2nd, pl., fut., act. indic.
19. 3rd, sg., fut. indic. (no voice for *fiō*)
20. 2nd, pl., pres., act. indic.
21. 1st, pl., fut., pass. indic.
22. 3rd, pl., pres., act. subj.
23. 1st, sg., fut., act. indic.
24. 2nd, sg., pres., act. subj.
25. 3rd, sg., pres., pass. subj.

SELECTION V

TRANSLATION

My woman says that she prefers to marry no one before me (wishes to marry no one more than me),
> Not if Jupiter himself should seek her.

She says (this): but whatever (that which) a woman says to a desirous (eager) lover
> It is necessary to (one should) write on the wind and rapid water.

SELECTION V

> **Mulier mea dīcit sē nullī quam mihi nūbere malle,**
> **nōn sī Iuppiter ipse sē petat.**
> **Dīcit: sed quod mulier cupidō amantī dīcit**
> **in ventō et rapidā aquā scrībere oportet.**

ANALYSIS AND COMPREHENSION OF THE LATIN TEXT

1. There is **ANAPHORA** of *dīcit* in lines 1 and 3.

LITERARY ANALYSIS AND DISCUSSION

1. **IRONY** appears in the poem in the humorous contrast between the *mulier*'s repeated words (*dīcit . . . dīcit* and the poet's realization that her repeated words are as lasting and meaningful as those in line 4, written in wind or swift wave (no permanence at all). There may also be a subtly humorous and **IRONIC** twist to the *mulier*'s stated preference of the poet to Jupiter himself (line 2) and the poet's statement that a woman's words to an eager lover (*cupidō amantī*) are worthless, since Jupiter is the example *par excellence* in legend and myth of an eager lover whose spoken words are singularly untrustworthy.

2. **ANAPHORA** is an effective device in this poem because it intensifies the contrast between the woman and her saying (*mulier dīcit* [line 1], *Dīcit* [line 3], *mulier dīcit* [line 3]) and the man and his writing (*amantī* [line 3] and *scrībere oportet* [line 4]). **HYPERBOLE** is an effective device in this poem because the exaggerated words of the woman (that she prefers to marry the poet to marrying the king of heaven (*Iuppiter ipse*) suggest that her other statements to him are equally exaggerated (and hence untrustworthy). See also #1 above.

RAPID REVIEW #5
PRACTICE

1. <u>How</u> beautiful/shapely/physcially attractive Lesbia was!
2. Maria is more beautiful <u>than</u> Quintia, but Lesbia is the most beautiful of all three.
3. Lucius is not quicker/swifter than Marcus, but he is <u>as</u> strong/brave <u>as possible</u>.
4. <u>What/Which</u> girl did Catullus love?
5. The girl <u>whom</u> Catullus loved was Lesbia.

SELECTION VI

TRANSLATION

    Farewell, girl! Now Catullus is firm,
    neither will he ask you back nor will he ask you (who are) unwilling.
    But you will feel pain, when you will be asked not at all.
    Wicked woman, damn you! What life remains for you?
5   Who now will visit you? To whom will you seem lovely?
    Whom now will you love? Whose will you be said to be?
    Whom will you kiss? Whose little lips will you nibble?
    But you, Catullus, having made up your mind, be firm!

SELECTION VI

> Valē, puella! Iam Catullus obdūrat,
> nec tē requīret nec tē invītam rogābit.
> At tū dolēbis, cum nihil rogāberis.
> Scelesta, vae tē! Quae vīta tibi manet?
> 5   Quis tē nunc adībit? Cui bella vidēberis?
> Quem nunc amābis? Cūius esse dīcēris?
> Quem bāsiābis? Cūius labella mordēbis?
> At tū, Catulle, destinātus obdūrā.

ANALYSIS AND COMPREHENSION OF THE LATIN TEXT

1. Catullus seems to have decided the relationship is finished and he should get on with life, putting Lesbia behind him. He says that his decision will cause her pain when no one pays any attention to her any more.
2. The presence of the *tū* adds great emphasis to the girl, for Latin normally employs the nominative case of personal pronouns only when clarity is needed or the writer/speaker wished to place stress on the subject.
3. The last six interrogative forms are pronouns (each has its own case, number and gender while line 4's *Quae* modifies *vīta*).
4. There are seven questions in lines 4–7, all rhetorical since they are asked for dramatic effect rather than to elicit information.
5. *Valē* and *obdūrā* are singular present imperatives.

LITERARY ANALYSIS AND DISCUSSION

1. A modern equivalent might be "Damn you!" or "Go to/Rot in hell!"
2. An effect of the piled-up questions in lines 4–7 is to highlight that the *puella* is anything but departed from his mind. The questions show that he is still remembering all the details of the former relationship.
3. The emotions, mood swings and contrasts may be caused by his pain over the end of their relationship. He says that he is in control and that it's over, that <u>she</u> will regret its end. His questions show <u>his</u> mentally uncontrolled nature, <u>his</u> regret and still vivid memories, but then he orders himself to regain and stay in control (*destinātus* and *obdūrā*).
4. *Destinātus* describes the mental state that the poet wants to be in, but the lines emphasize that he is not always in that state.

RAPID REVIEW #6
PRACTIVE A.

1. What (neuter, pl.) is my woman saying?
2. Who prefers to marry me?
3. What (sg.) did my woman say?
4. What/which evil men can be jealous?
5. Whose words ought to be written on the wind?
6. With whose (fem. pl.) fingers are Lesbia's fingers compared?
7. With whom (pl.) is my Lesbia being compared?
8. By whom (sg.) is that girl said to be beautiful?
9. With what/which girls is my Lesbia compared?
10. To whom (pl.) in the province are these things being told? To whom (sg.) has my girl said these things?

PRACTICE B

1. (IP) *Quem, Quōs* or *Quās*
2. (IP) *Quae* (neuter, pl.)
3. (IP) *Quōcum* or *Quibuscum*
4. (IP) *Quō* or *Quibus*
5. (IP) *Ā cuius* or *quōrum* or *quārum amīcō*
6. (IA) *Ad quam puellam*
7. (IA) *Quā in terrā/patriā*
8. (IP) *Cuius* or *Quōrum* or *Quārum*
9. (IP) *Cui* or *Quibus*
10. (IP) *Ad quem* or *Ad quōs*

MAJOR REVIEW #1

INFINITIVES

I. DRILL

A.

1. basiāre – to kiss   basiārī – to be kissed   basiāvisse – to have kissed
   basiātus, -a, -um esse – to have been kissed   basiātūrus, -a, -um esse – to be about to kiss
2. mordēre – to bite   mordērī – to be bitten   momordisse – to have bitten
   morsus, -a, -um esse – to have been bitten   morsūrus, -a, -um esse – to be about to bite
3. tegere – to cover   tegī – to be covered   texisse – to have covered
   tectus, -a, -um esse – to have been covered   tectūrus, -a, -um esse – to be about to cover
4. surripere – to steal   surripī – to be stolen   surripuisse – to have stolen
   surreptus, -a, -um esse – to have been stolen   surreptūrus, -a, -um esse – to be about to steal
5. audīre – to hear   audīrī – to be heard   audīvisse – to have heard
   audītus, -a, -um esse – to have been heard   audītūrus, -a, -um esse – to be about to hear

B.

1. present active – to love
2. present passive – to be warned
3. perfect active – to have said
4. perfect passive – to have been seized
5. future active – to be about to know
6. present passive – to be known
7. future active – to be about to seize
8. present active – to say
9. perfect passive – to have been warned
10. perfect active – to have loved
11. present passive – to be loved
12. perfect active – to have warned
13. future active – to be about to say
14. present active – to seize
15. perfect passive – to have been known
16. perfect active – to have seized
17. present active – to warn
18. present active – to know
19. future active – to be about to love
20. perfect passive – to have been said
21. perfect passive – to have been loved
22. future active – to be about to warn
23. present passive – to be said
24. present passive – to be seized
25. perfect active – to have known

II. DRILL

1. *laudārī* – present passive; complementary to *dēbent*.
   Good girls ought to be praised.
2. *nubere* – present active; complementary to *mavult*.
   My woman prefers to marry me.

3. *dīcere* – present active; subject of *est. agere* – present active; subject of implied *est.*

   It is easy to say, difficult to do. Saying is easy, doing difficult.

4. *occidere* et *resurgere* – present active; complementary to *possunt.*

   Suns are able to (can) set and rise again.

5. *spectārī* – present passive; infinitive phrase *suam . . . spectārī* is object of *cupīvit.*

   She did not desire her daughter to be watched by all the boys.

6. *esse* – present active; infinitive phrase *suōs . . . esse sānōs* is object of *cupiunt.*

   Father and mother desire their sons to be healthy.

7. *dēcipere* is present active; infinitive phrase *Amīcum dēcipere* is subject of *est.*

   To deceive a friend is disgraceful. It is disgraceful to deceive a friend.

8. *facere* is present active; complementary to *dēbuit.*

   The bad boy should not have (ought not to have) done that.

9. *esse* – present active; complementary to *vidētur.*

   That one (He) seems to me to be equal to a god.

10. *dēpōnere* – present active; infinitive phrase *longum . . . amōrem* is subject of *est.*

    It is difficult suddenly to lay aside a long-time love. Suddenly to lay aside a long-time love is difficult.

III. DRILL A

1. Catullus says/is saying (today) that he loves Lesbia (today).
2. Catullus says/is saying (today) that he loved Lesbia (yesterday).
3. Catullus says/is saying (today) that he will/is going to love Lesbia (tomorrow).
4. Catullus says/is saying (today) that Lesbia is (being) loved by him (today).
5. Catullus says/is saying (today) that Lesbia was loved by him (yesterday).
6. The poet wrote (yesterday) that he was in love with/loved Lesbia (yesterday).
7. The poet wrote (yesterday) that he had been in love with/had loved Lesbia (the day before).
8. The poet wrote (yesterday) that he would be in love with/ was going to love Lesbia (today, tomorrow, always).
9. The poet wrote (yesterday) that Lesbia was being loved by him (yesterday).
10. The poet wrote (yesterday) that Lesbia had been loved by him (the day before).
11. Cornelius used to think that my scribblings were something (i.e. amounted to something, had some value).
12. Catullus thought that thousands of verses had been written (to excess) by Sufffenus.
13. My girl (friend) promised that she would give the choicest writings of the worst poet to the lame god.
14. Was the Province saying that the Formian's girl (friend) was beautiful?
15. Lesbia once upon a time was saying/used to say that she had loved Catullus alone/only Catullus.
16. Catullus considered/thought that he was true and had not violated (nor had he violated) a sacred vow.
17. No woman can/is able to say truly that she has been/was loved as much as my Lesbia has been/was loved by me.
18. You offer to/promise me, my Lesbia, that this love of ours will be/is going to be between us and eternal.
19. Catullus considered/thought that the poem had been charmingly begun/started by Caecilius.
20. The poet said that Pollio's brother had used his left hand not prettily/charmingly. (He had stolen one of the poet's table napkins).

MAJOR REVIEW 1

III. DRILL B

Selection I, lines 1-2: *esse* and *superāre* are present active and complementary to *vidētur*.

Selection II, line 5: *esse* is present active and used in indirect statement.

Selection III, line 4: *esse* is present active and used in indirect statement.

Selection IV, line 4: *occidere* and *resurgere* are present active and complementary to *possunt*.

lines 10–13: *invidēre* is present active and complementary to *possit*; *esse* is present active and used in indirect statement.

Selection V, line 1: *nūbere* is present active and complementary to *malle*; *malle* is present active and used in indirect statement.

line 4: *scrībere* is present active and used as the subject of *oportet*.

SELECTION VII

TRANSLATION

      You avoid me like a fawn, Chloe,
      seeking her quaking mother
      on pathless mountains not without a vain
      fear of the breezes and forest.

5   For whether the arrival of spring
      has rustled in the moving leaves
      or green lizards have moved apart the bramble,
      she trembles both in heart and knees.

      BUT I do not pursue you to break you,
10   like a fierce tigress or Gaetulian lion:
      (you who are) ripe for a man, finally cease
      to follow your mother.

SELECTION VII

> Vītās mē inuleō similis, Chloē,
> quaerentī pavidam mātrem
> montibus āviīs nōn sine vānō
> metū aurārum et silvae.
>
> 5   Nam seu adventus vēris
> foliīs mobilibus inhorruit,
> seu viridēs lacertae rubum dīmōvērunt,
> et corde et genibus tremit.
>
> Atquī nōn ego tē frangere persequor,
> 10 ut tigris aspera Gaetūlusve leō:
> tandem dēsine, tempestīva virō,
> mātrem sequī.

ANALYSIS AND COMPREHENSION OF THE LATIN TEXT

1. The skittish fawn fears being alone on the pathless mountains and is startled by natural events (e.g. a breeze) in its natural home, the forest. The doe, its mother, fears that its offspring may come to harm. Chloe seems to fear the poet/lover.
2. *Nōn sine* (instead of *cum*) exemplifies the **LITOTES** in line 3.
3. The indications of spring's arrival in lines 5–8 are the moving leaves and the movement of the lizards as they poke their way through the brambles. The words associated with movement are *mōbilibus, inhorruit, dīmōvērunt* and *tremit*.

LITERARY ANALYSIS AND DISCUSSION

1. The fawn's fear (*metū*) in the unfamiliar setting (*montibus āviīs*) of both a natural event (*aurārum*) and of its natural habitat (*silvae*) may parallel a youngster's uncertainties and fears as he/she matures and experiences for the first time natural events, feelings and changes in his/her life. The mother's fear (*pavidam matrem*) for her maturing offspring as she goes off to explore on her own may parallel a human mother's anxiety for her child as she/he becomes more independent and adventuresome. Parental fears and parameters are, it seems, timeless.
2. The body's internal and external quaking (*tremit*, line 8) could be the child's fears for herself/himself or the mother's for the child's safety and well-being.
3. The fragility of a "twig" is perhaps highlighted by the idea of breaking in *frangere*. Alternatively, it is also true that a "young shoot, twig" is unusually pliant and flexible, harder to break off than a somewhat older small branch.

RAPID REVIEW #7

1. Enclitic: -ne. <u>You</u> the province says to be beautiful? The province claims that <u>you</u> are beautiful?
2. Enclitic: -ve. . . . a fierce tigress or Gaetulian lion . . .
3. Enclitic: -que. What upper arms I saw and touched!
4. Enclitic: -que. A lover will go into mountains and deep rivers.
5. Enclitic: -que. I sing of arms and a man.
6. Enclitic: -ne. Is there such great anger to heavenly spirits (Do heavenly spirits have such great wrath)?
7. Enclitic: -ne. Was Pallas able to set on fire the Argive (Greek) fleet?
8. Enclitic -que. The city was rich in resources and very fierce in the pursuits of war.
9. Enclitic: -ne. Did such a great confidence in your birth seize you?
10. Enclitic: -met. Be firm, and save your very own selves for favorable times/matters/situations.

SELECTION VIII - A & B

TRANSLATION

"As long as I was pleasing/welcome to you
nor was some preferable youth
giving his arms to your fair/white neck,
I flourished more blessed than a king of the Persians."

5 "As long as you did not burn more because of another
nor was Lydia behind Chloe,
Lydia of much renown,
I flourished more famous/bright than Roman Ilia."

"Thracian Chloe now rules me,
10 learned in sweet measures and knowledgeable of the lyre,
for whom I will not fear to die,
if the fates spare her life/my darling and let her survive."

"Calais, the son of Ornytus from Thurii,
burns me with a shared torch,
15 for whom I will endure dying twice,
if the fates spare the boy and let him survive."

"What if old Love returns
and forces the separated ones under a bronze yoke?
If fiery Chloe is shaken out
20 and the door of/to rejected Lydia stands open?"

"Although he is more handsome than a star,
you more fickle than a cork and more hot-tempered
than the rough Adriatic Sea, with you I would love to live,
with you I would willingly die."

"Donec tibi grātus eram
nec quisquam iuvenis potior
bracchia candidae cervīcī dabat,
beātior Persārum rēge viguī."

5   "Donec aliā nōn magis arsistī
neque Lȳdia post Chloēn erat,
Lȳdia multī nōminis,
clārior Rōmānā Īliā viguī."

"Thressa Chloē mē nunc regit,
10 docta dulcēs modōs et citharae sciēns,
prō quā morī nōn metuam,
sī fāta animae superstitī parcent."

"Calais, fīlius Thūrīnī Ornytī,
face mūtuā mē torret,
15 prō quō bis morī patiar,
sī fāta puerō superstitī parcent."

"Quid sī prisca Venus redit
dīductōsque iugō aēneō cōgit?
Sī flāva Chloē excutitur
20 reiectaeque Lȳdiae iānua patet?"

"Quamquam sīdere pulchrior ille est,
tū levior cortice et īrācundior
improbō Hadriā, tēcum vīvere amem,
tēcum libēns obeam."

ANALYSIS AND COMPREHENSION OF THE LATIN TEXT

1. The personal names are Lydia, Chloe, Calais, Ornytus, Ilia and Venus. The initial three are involved in the poem's dramatic situation, but the name of the male lover (the poet??) is absent.
2. The "old Love" refers to Lydia (as well as the obvious deity).
3. In form the phrase can be either case. If it is taken as dative, then the male retains some control of the situation, opening the *iānua* to/for Lydia. If it is taken as genitive, Lydia has control as it is her door that she opens up to her former lover.
4. The reader is expected to supply an *es* as the verb for *tū*.

LITERARY ANALYSIS AND DISCUSSION

1. The name of the male lover – the poet? – is absent, possibly implying that the entire scenario presented in the poem is imaginary. (This may be an appropriate time to discuss the difference between the poet in his real life and the poet's literary *persona*.)
2. Themes of a masculine focus on power and control in contrast to a feminine search for popularity and passion remain widespread in contemporary culture (literature, musical lyrics and videos, films, including pornography) and society. Students often readily identify similar attitudes in their own experiences in and out of the school setting.
3. *Aliā* means "one, another" (from a group of three or more) while the reference in *altera* is restricted to a group of two. Consequently, Lydia may be suggesting that the unnamed male, her "ex," had been involved with other women than Chloe and herself.
4. The reference to a *fax*, possibly a wedding torch, may suggest that Lydia and Calais were talking of marriage. Alternatively, the erotic and Freudian symbolism of a "shared torch" (*face mutuā*), suggesting the degree of the new lovers' intimacy, may arise in a class discussion.

SELECTION VIII-A & B

RAPID REVIEW #8
PRACTICE 1.

ager latior	domus latior	flūmen latius
agrī latiōris	domūs/domī latiōris	flūminis latiōris
agrō latiōrī	domuī/domō latiōrī	flūminī latiōrī
agrum latiōrem	domum latiōrem	flūmen latius
agrō latiōre	domū/domō latiōre	flūmine latiōre
agrī latiōrēs	domūs latiōrēs	flūmina latiōra
agrōrum latiōrum	domuum/domōrum latiōrum	flūminum latiōrum
agrīs latiōribus	domibus latiōribus	flūminibus latiōribus
agrōs latiōrēs	domūs/domōs latiōrēs	flūmina latiōra
agrīs latiōribus	domibus latiōribus	flūminibus latiōribus

PRACTICE 2.

	asperior, asperius	asperrimus, -a, -um
beātus, -a, -um		beātissimus, -a, -um
bonus, -a, -um	melior, melius	
	brevior, brevius	brevissimus, -a, -um
facilis, -e		facillimus, -a, -um
grātus, -a, -um	grātior, grātius	
	miserior, miserius	miserrimus, -a, -um
mōbilis, -e		mōbilissimus, -a, -um
niger, -gra, -grum	nigrior, nigrius	
	minor, minus	minimus, -a, -um
pulcher, -chra, -chrum		pulcherrimus, -a, -um
similis, -e	similior, similius	

RAPID REVIEW #9

1. Simple Condition. If the fates spare his life, Lydia does not fear to die.
2. Simple Condition. If the fates (will) spare his life, Lydia will not fear to die.
3. S/W Condition. If the fates should spare his life, Lydia would not fear to die.
4. CF-present Condition. If the fates were to spare his life, Lydia would not fear to die.
5. CF-past Condition. If the fates had spared his life, Lydia would not have feared to die.
6. Simple Condition. If the former Love does not return, fiery Chloe is not shaken out/jilted.
7. Simple Condition. If the former Love will not return, fiery Chloe will not be shaken out/jilted.
8. S/W Condition. If the former Love should not return, fiery Chloe would not be shaken out/jilted.
9. CF-present Condition. If the former Love were not to return, fiery Chloe would not be shaken out/jilted.
10. CF-past Condition. If the former Love had not returned, fiery Chloe would not have been shaken out/jilted.

11. Simple condition. If you have good character, we praise you.
12. Simple condition. If you (will) have good character, we shall praise you.
13. S/W condition. If you should have good character, we would praise you.
14. CF-present condition. If you were to have good character, we would praise you.
15. CF-past condition. If you had had good character, we would have praised you.
16. Simple condition. If we do not seek truth, we do not find wisdom.
17. Simple condition. If we do (will) not seek truth, we shall not find wisdom.
18. S/W condition. If we should not seek truth, we would not find wisdom.
19. CF-present condition. If we were not seeking truth, we would not find wisdom.
20. CF-past condition. If we had not sought truth, we would not have found wisdom.

SELECTION IX

TRANSLATION (Note alternate version of final two lines.)

I until recently lived fit for the girls
and I soldiered on not without glory.
Now this wall will hold my gear/weapons
and my lyre retired from war,

5   (the wall) which guards the left side
of sea-born Venus. Here, right here put
the burning torches and crowbars and bows
(which are) threatening to blocking doors (doors placed as opposition).

O goddess, you who hold blessed Cyprus
10   and Memphis lacking Sithonian snow,
O queen, touch just this once scornful Chloe
    (O queen, touch with your uplifted whip)
with your uplifted whip.
    (Chloe, [because she is being] scornful just this once.)

SELECTION IX

> Vīxī nūper idōneus puellīs
> et mīlitāvī nōn sine glōriā.
> Nunc hic pariēs arma habēbit
> dēfunctumque bellō barbiton,
>
> 5   quī laevum marīnae Veneris latus
> custōdit. Hīc, hīc pōnite
> lūcida fūnālia et vectēs et arcūs
> oppositīs foribus mināces.
>
> Ō dīva, quae beātum Cyprum tenēs
> 10   et Memphin Sīthoniā nive carentem,
> Ō rēgīna, sublīmī flagellō tange
> Chloēn semel arrogantem.

ANALYSIS AND COMPREHENSION OF THE LATIN TEXT

1. The phrase *nōn sine glōriā* is an example of **LITOTES**, *hīc, hīc* of **ANAPHORA** and *bellō barbiton* of **ALLITERATION**.
2. In lines 7–8, *arcūs . . . mināces* form a **CHIASMUS**. In line 10, *Memphin . . . carentem* form a **CHIASMUS**.
3. The lover's weapons suggest that he was an infantryman, though the specialized *vectēs* may suggest a Special Forces (e.g. U. S. Ranger) type.

LITERARY ANALYSIS AND DISCUSSION

1. The Thracian connotation in *Sīthoniā nīve* picks up on *Threissa Chloe* in line 9 of Selection VIII–A. If the Chloes of Selections VII–IX are the same, the fearful fawn of VII seems to have replaced Lydia as the poet's lover in VIII and no longer to be interested in him in IX.
2. A possible response concerning the **METAPHOR**'s effectiveness might include the observations that the **METAPHOR** is sustained by
   a. lines 1–2 which state that the poet's <u>past</u> (*nūper*) campaign as a soldier in the battles of love had been very successful (*mīlitāvī nōn sine glōriā*);
   b. line 3 which describe the <u>present</u> (*nunc*) situation and the <u>future</u> retirement from active duty (*habē<u>bit</u>*).
3. a. The strong imperative form instead of the milder subjunctive form may show the man's impatience at the current situation.
   b. Some readers think that the poet may seek punishment for the girl for her disinterest in him (hence offending Venus, the goddess of passion). Other readers note that *tange* suggests merely "touching" with the whip, and suggest that a painful punishment may be too strong an idea, They suggest that the aim of his plea to the *dea* is the return of Chloe to his embrace, and consequently read the poem more light-heartedly.

4. *semel*'s possible meanings (one time only; once and for all; for the first time; at some time) allow richly ambiguous readings. If read with *tange*, the phrase could mean

    touch only once (I don't want her hurt.)

    touch once and for all (that's all she'll need)

    touch for the first time (she's not been reluctant before)

    touch at some time in the future (but I'm OK for now)

    If read with *arrogantem*, the phrase could mean

    because she's become arrogant (scornful of me) this time

    because she's become arrogant (scornful of me) once and for all

    because she's become arrogant (scornful of me) for the first time

    because she'll become arrogant (scornful of me) at some time in the future

5. A reader's understanding of the poet's seriousness in saying farewell to love's battles will vary with his/her interpretation of the last stanza (see numbers 3 & 4).

RAPID REVIEW #10
PRACTICE A. Synopses

hortor	confitēris	ūtitur	patimur	experiuntur
hortābar	confitēbāris	ūtēbātur	patiēbāmur	experiēbantur
hortābor	confitēberis	ūtētur	patiēmur	experientur
hortātus sum	confessus es	ūsus est	passī sumus	expertī sunt
hortātus eram	confessus erās	ūsus erat	passī erāmus	expertī erant
hortātus erō	confessus eris	ūsus erit	passī erimus	expertī erunt
horter	confiteāris	ūtātur	patiāmur	experiantur
hortārer	confitērēris	ūterētur	paterēmur	experīrentur
hortātus sim	confessus sīs	ūsus sit	passī sīmus	expertī sint
hortātus essem	confessus essēs	ūsus esset	passī essēmus	expertī essent

PRACTICE B. Participles and Infinitives

sequēns (sequentis) – following

secūtus, -a, -um – having followed

secūtūrus, -a, -um – about to follow

sequendus, -a, -um – about to be followed

sequī – to follow

secūtus, -a, -um esse – to have followed

secūtūrus, -a, -um esse – to be about to follow

PRACTICE C.

1. I admit/confess/allow these things like this one-by-one/individually.
2. This wall will have/hold my arms and retired lyre.
3. Not I follow (you) to crush/break you. I do not follow . . .
4. At last/finally stop following/cease to follow your mother.
5. Night has gone away and day has not yet arisen/nor has day yet arisen.

MAJOR REVIEW #2

Form Drill

1.

  a. dans – giving
     datus, -a, um – (having been) given
     datūrus, -a, -um – about to give
     dandus, -a, -um – about to be given

  b. torrēns – burning
     tostus, -a, -um – (having been) burned
     tostūrus, -a, -um – about to burn
     torrendus, -a, -um – about to be burned

  c. regēns – ruling
     rectus, -a, -um – (having been) ruled
     rectūrus, -a, -um – about to rule
     regendus, -a, -um – about to be ruled

  d. excutiēns – shaking out
     excussus, -a, -um – (having been) shaken out
     excussūrus, -a, -um – about to shake out
     excutiendus, -a, -um – about to be shaken out

  e. patiēns – enduring
     passus, -a, -um – having endured
     passūrus, -a, -um – about to endure
     patiendus, -a, -um – about to be endured

2.

  a. present active – avoiding
  b. perfect passive – (having been) taught
  c. future active – about to break
  d. future passive – about to be followed
  e. present active – guarding
  f. perfect passive – (having been) avoided
  g. future active – about to teach
  h. future passive – about to be broken
  i. present active – following
  j. perfect passive – (having been) guarded
  k. future active – about to avoid
  l. future passive – about to be taught
  m. present active – breaking
  n. perfect active – having followed
  o. future active – about to guard
  p. future passive – about to be avoided
  q. present active – teaching
  r. perfect passive – (having been) broken
  s. future active – about to follow
  t. future passive – about to be guarded

REGULAR ADJECTIVAL MODIFIER DRILL

1. Who was the man sitting opposite Lesbia? Who was the man who was sitting opposite Lesbia?
2. I was able to hear Lesbia laughing sweetly. I could hear Lesbia as she laughed sweetly.
3. The girl, having neither a graceful/dainty foot nor dark eyes, should not be compared with our Lesbia. The girl who has/because she has neither a graceful foot nor dark eyes, ought not to be compared with our Lesbia.
4. Catullus, denying that Quintia was lovely/beautiful/shapely, kept praising Lesbia. Catullus, while he denied that Quintia was lovely, kept praising Lesbia.
5. Let us ourselves, estimating that the rumors of the old men are worth (only) an *as*, live and love! Let us ourselves, because we estimate the rumors of the old men to be worth (only) an *as*, live and love!
6. A woman, saying that she prefers to wed no one more than her lover, is not always believable. A woman, who says/when she says that she prefers to marry no one before her lover, is not always credible.
7. The wicked girl, (having been) asked not at all, will suffer pain/grieve. The wicked girl, when/because/if she has not been invited at all, will feel pain.
8. The girl will not be asked by Catullus, now being firm – and will suffer pain. The girl will not be asked by Catullus who/because he now is being tough – and she will suffer.
9. Chloe, seeking her mother, avoided the poet. Chloe, when she sought her mother, avoided the poet.
10. The mother was sought by the fawn, having a vain fear of the breezes. The doe was sought by the fawn who/because she had an empty/insubstantial fear of the breezes.

ABLATIVE ABSOLUTE DRILL

1. You having been seen, Lesbia, my tongue is numb. After/since you have been seen, Lesbia, my tongue grows numb.
2. Lesbia having been compared with you, the age is truly unwise and lacking in taste! If Lesbia has been compared with you, the generation is truly tasteless and clueless!
3. Quintia having been denied to be beautiful/shapely/lovely, Lesbia was praised by all. After/Since Quintia had been denied to be lovely, Lesbia was praised by all.
4. All the rumors of the old men having been reckoned as worth an *as*, let us live and love! Because all the rumors of the old men have been valued at an *as*, let us live and love!
5. Many thousands of kisses having been made, may no evil man be able to be envious of us. When/After/Because many thousand kisses have been made, no evil man should envy us.
6. A man being desirous, a woman is not to be believed. When a man is full of desire, a woman must/should not be believed.
7. Catullus having been made tough, the girl will grieve. Because Catullus has been made tough, the girl will suffer.
8. The fawn, the brambles having been moved aside by the lizards, trembles in both heart and knees. When the brambles have been parted by the lizards, the fawn quakes both in its heart and knees.
9. No youth being preferable to you, I lived/flourished more blessed than the king of the Persians. When/While/as long as no young man was preferable to you, I flourished more blessed than the king of the Persians.
10. The son of Ornytus setting me ablaze, I will suffer dying twice. If the son of Ornytus lights my fire, I will endure death twice.

MAJOR REVIEW 2

PERIPHRASTIC DRILL

1. Quintia is not to be (should not be/must not be) compared with our Lesbia.
2. Lesbia was to be/had to be praised by all.
3. If the fates are going to spare the boy, I am going to suffer dying twice.
4. All the rumors of the old men should be (must be/have to be) valued at an *as*.
5. All things, which a woman says to a desirous lover, must be written on the wind and swift water by you, Catullus.
6. The wicked girl's little lips should be (must be/ought to be) kissed by no one.
7. Your mother must not be followed by you, Chloe, (who are) fit for a man.
8. This wall is about to hold/going to have my weapons.
9. The door of Lydia standing open, fiery Chloe must be shaken out/jilted. If the door, When the door, Because the door . . .
10. Chloe, O Queen, must be (has to be, should be) touched with uplifted whip.

REVIEW DRILL

Sel. I. 1–5: *sedēns* is present active and nominative, singular, masculine, modifying *quī*. It is used as a <u>R</u>egular <u>A</u>djectival <u>M</u>odifier (here after RAM).

rīdentem is present active and accusative, singular, feminine, modifying *tē*. It is used as a RAM.

Sel. V. 3–4: *amantī* is present active and dative, singular, masculine. It is a RAM used substantively.

Sel. VI. 8: *dēstinātus* is perfect passive and nominative, singular, masculine, modifying *tū*. It is used as a RAM.

Sel. VII. 1–4: *quaerentī* is present active and dative, singular, masculine, modifying *inuleō*. It is used as a RAM.

Sel. VIII-A. 9–12: *docta* is perfect passive and nominative, singular and feminine, modifying *Chloē*. It is used as a RAM.

sciēns is present active and nominative, singular and feminine, modifying *Chloē*. It is used as a RAM.

Sel. VIII-B. 17–18: *dīductōs* is perfect passive and accusative, plural, masculine, modifying an understood *eōs*. It is used as a RAM.

21–24: *libēns* is present active and nominative, singular and feminine, modifying the subject of *obeam*. It is used as a RAM.

Sel. IX. 3–4: *dēfunctum* is perfect, passive (deponent) and accusative, singular and neuter, modifying *barbiton*. It is used as a RAM.

6–8: *oppositīs* is perfect passive and dative, plural and masculine, modifying *foribus*. It is used as a RAM.

9–12: *carentem* and *arrogantem* are present active and accusative, singular and feminine, modifying *Memphin* and *Chloēn*, respectively. Each is used as a RAM.

SELECTION X - A & B (EXPURGATED)

TRANSLATION

    It was hot, and the day had passed the middle hour;
        I placed my limbs (about) to be relieved in the middle of the bed.
    Part of the window was opened, the other part (was) closed,
        the sort of light woods generally are accustomed to have,
5   the sort of twilight that shines faintly when Phoebus is fleeing
        or when night has gone nor yet has day risen.
    That light must be provided to bashful girls
        in which timid modesty may hope to have hiding places.
    Look! Corinna comes, dressed in a loosened tunic,
10   with her parted hair covering her fair neck,
    just like shapely Semiramis is said to have gone into bedrooms,
        and Lais (who was) loved by many men.
    I tore off the tunic; nor was the scanty thing doing much harm
        but she still was struggling to be covered by the tunic;
15   and since/when she was struggling like a woman who would not wish to overcome,
        she was overcome not with difficulty by her own betrayal/treason.
    As she stood there before our eyes with the garment laid aside,
        nowhere on her whole body was there a flaw.
        . . . .
20   . . . .
        . . . .
        . . . .
    Individual features – why should I repeat them? I saw nothing not praiseworthy,
        and I pressed the nude girl tightly to my own body.
25   Who does not know the rest? Worn out, we began to rest up – both of us.
        May mid-days like this often happen for me!

Aestus erat, et diēs mediam hōram exēgerat;
  adposuī mediō membra levanda torō.
Pars fenestrae adaperta fuit, pars altera clausa,
  quāle lūmen silvae habēre ferē solent,
5 quālia crepuscula sublūcent Phoebō fugiente
  aut ubi nox abiit nec tamen diēs orta.
Illa lux verēcundīs puellīs est praebenda,
  quā timidus pudor latebrās habēre spēret.
Ecce! Corinna venit, tunicā vēlāta recinctā,
10 dīviduā comā candida colla tegente,
quāliter in thalamōs fāmōsa Semiramis īsse
  dīcitur et Lāis multīs amāta virīs.
Dēripuī tunicam; nec multum rāra nocēbat
  sed illa tamen tunicā tegī pugnābat;
15 quae cum ita pugnāret tamquam quae vincere nollet,
  victa est nōn aegrē prōditiōne suā.
Ut stetit ante oculōs nostrōs positō vēlāmine,
  nusquam in tōtō corpore menda fuit.
  . . . .
20 . . . .
  . . . .
  . . . .
Singula quid referam? Nil nōn laudābile vīdī,
  et nūdam pressī usque ad corpus meum.
25 Cētera quis nescit? Lassī requiēvimus ambō.
  Mediī diēs sīc mihi saepe prōveniant!

ANALYSIS AND COMPREHENSION OF THE LATIN TEXT

1. The words *fenestrae* and *fuit* are to be inferred from the first half of the line.
2. The eight participles are:

    levanda – Regular Adjectival Modifier

    fugiente – Ablative Absolute

    praebenda – Passive Periphrastic

    vēlāta – Regular Adjectival Modifier

    recinctā – Regular Adjectival Modifier

    tegente – Ablative Absolute

    amāta – Regular Adjectival Modifier

    positō – Ablative Absolute

3. The *membra levanda* are in the middle of the bed.
4. There is **ALLITERATION** of the *m* sound (*mediō membra*) in line 2 and of the *c* sound (*coma candidā colla*) in line 10. There is **METONYMY** in the poet's use in line 5 of *Phoebō* to represent *sōl*. **CHIASMUS** is found in line 10's *comā . . . tegente*. **SYNCHESIS** is found in line 12's *Lāis multīs amāta virīs*.
5. The *tunica* was likely a lingerie-type "robe."
6. The plural nouns highlight the active sex lives of these famous women.
7. **HYPERBOLE** is present in line 18's description of Corinna's physical perfection. **LITOTES** exists in line 16's *nōn aegrē*. **ANAPHORA** is present in the repeated QU exclamatory words in lines 19–22.
8. The *cum* clause in line 15 most likely expresses cause.
9. *Singula quid referam?* is a deliberative question, while *Cētera quis nescit?* is a rhetorical question.

LITERARY ANALYSIS AND DISCUSSION

1. The implication of Corinna's hair being "down" (loosened, flowing) as opposed to "up" is that she is not portrayed as a "proper" Roman woman. More likely, she was a courtesan. The fact that she is compared to Greek (Lais) and Middle Eastern (Semiramis) women may suggest an exotic (to a Roman) foreigner. Such residents in Rome at that time typically were war slaves or freedwomen. There was a Greek lyric poetess named Corinna who lived and wrote in the 5th century BCE and is often associated with the more famous poet Pindar. Consequently, Corinna may be a "professional" or "stage" name for a woman who was Rome's equivalent of a talented "geisha" or "escort."
2. That she came to his residence (line 9), had an already loosened robe (line 9), had her hair undone (line 10), wore a *tunica* that was *rara* (line 13) and was resisting like one who did not wish to win the struggle (line 15) may support the insincerity of her resistance. On the other hand, it is he who provides these details and observations, so it is his view of events.
3. The plural possessive adjective *nostrōs* (rather than *meōs*) may suggest that Corinna as well as the poet admired the appearance of her uncovered body. The *ambō* ("both") in line 25 also suggests a shared pleasure in the encounter.

SELECTION X - A & B (UNEXPURGATED)

In this rather specific poem, Ovid describes a summer afternoon's enjoyable siesta. He sets the scene, describes Corinna's coming—and what follows. The poem's twenty-six lines have been divided into two assignments or sections: lines 1–12 in SELECTION X-A and lines 13–26 in SELECTION X-B.

TRANSLATION

    It was hot, and the day had passed the middle hour;
        I placed my limbs (about) to be relieved in the middle of the bed.
    Part of the window was opened, the other part (was) closed,
        the sort of light woods generally are accustomed to have,
5   the sort of twilight that shines faintly when Phoebus is fleeing
        or when night has gone nor yet has day risen.
    That light must be provided to bashful girls
        in which timid modesty may hope to have hiding places.
    Look! Corinna comes, dressed in a loosened tunic,
10   with her parted hair covering her fair neck,
    just like shapely Semiramis is said to have gone into bedrooms,
        and Lais (who was) loved by many men.
    I tore off the tunic; nor was the scanty thing doing much harm
        but she still was struggling to be covered by the tunic;
15   and since/when she was struggling like a woman who would not wish to overcome,
        she was overcome not with difficulty by her own betrayal/treason.
    As she stood there before our eyes with the garment laid aside,
        nowhere on her whole body was there a flaw:
    what shoulders, what sort of upper arms did I see and touch!
20   How fit to be pressed was the shape of her breasts!
    How flat her tummy beneath her firm chest!
        The size and quality of her flank! How youthful her thigh!
    Individual features – why should I repeat them? I saw nothing not praiseworthy,
        and I pressed the nude girl tightly to my own body.
25   Who does not know the rest? Worn out, we began to rest up – both of us.
        May mid-days like this often happen for me!

Aestus erat, et diēs mediam hōram exēgerat;
  adposuī mediō membra levanda torō.
Pars fenestrae adaperta fuit, pars altera clausa,
  quāle lūmen silvae habēre ferē solent,
5 quālia crepuscula sublūcent Phoebō fugiente
  aut ubi nox abiit nec tamen diēs orta.
Illa lux verēcundīs puellīs est praebenda,
  quā timidus pudor latebrās habēre spēret.
Ecce! Corinna venit, tunicā vēlāta recinctā,
10 dīviduā comā candida colla tegente,
quāliter in thalamōs fāmōsa Semiramis īsse
  dīcitur et Lāis multīs amāta virīs.
Dēripuī tunicam; nec multum rāra nocēbat
  sed illa tamen tunicā tegī pugnābat;
15 quae cum ita pugnāret tamquam quae vincere nollet,
  victa est nōn aegrē prōditiōne suā.
Ut stetit ante oculōs nostrōs positō vēlāmine,
  nusquam in tōtō corpore menda fuit:
quōs umerōs, quālēs vīdī tetigīque lacertōs!
20 Forma papillārum quam apta premī fuit!
Quam plānus venter sub pectore castīgātō!
  Quantum et quāle latus! Quam iuvenāle femur!
Singula quid referam? Nil nōn laudābile vīdī,
  et nūdam pressī usque ad corpus meum.
25 Cētera quis nescit? Lassī requiēvimus ambō.
  Mediī diēs sīc mihi saepe prōveniant!

ANALYSIS AND COMPREHENSION OF THE LATIN TEXT

1. The words *fenestrae* and *fuit* are to be inferred from the first half of the line.

2. The eight participles are:

   levanda – Regular Adjectival Modifier

   fugiente – Ablative Absolute

   praebenda – Passive Periphrastic

   vēlāta – Regular Adjectival Modifier

   recinctā – Regular Adjectival Modifier

   tegente – Ablative Absolute

   amāta – Regular Adjectival Modifier

   positō – Ablative Absolute

3. The *membra levanda* are in the middle of the bed.

4. There is **ALLITERATION** of the *m* sound (*mediō membra*) in line 2 and of the *c* sound (*coma candidā colla*) in line 10. There is **METONYMY** in the poet's use in line 5 of *Phoebō* to represent *sōl*. **CHIASMUS** is found in line 10's *comā . . . tegente*. **SYNCHESIS** is found in line 12's *Lāis multīs amāta virīs*.

5. The *tunica* was likely a lingerie-type "robe."

6. The plural nouns highlight the active sex lives of these famous women.

7. **ANAPHORA** is present in the repeated QU exclamatory words in lines 19–22. **HYPERBOLE** is present in line 18's description of Corinna's physical perfection. **LITOTES** exists in line 16's *nōn aegrē*.

8. The *cum* clause in line 15 most likely expresses cause.

9. *Singula quid referam?* is a deliberative question, while *Cētera quis nescit?* is a rhetorical question.

LITERARY ANALYSIS AND DISCUSSION

1. The implication of Corinna's hair being "down" (loosened, flowing) as opposed to "up" is that she is not portrayed as a "proper" Roman woman. More likely, she was a courtesan. The fact that she is compared to Greek (Lais) and Middle Eastern (Semiramis) women may suggest an exotic (to a Roman) foreigner. Such residents in Rome at that time typically were war slaves or freedwomen. There was a Greek lyric poetess named Corinna who lived and wrote in the 5th century BCE and is often associated with the more famous poet Pindar. Consequently, Corinna may be a "professional" or "stage" name for a woman who was Rome's equivalent of a talented "geisha" or "escort."

2. That she came to his residence (line 9), had an already loosened robe (line 9), had her hair undone (line 10), wore a *tunica* that was *rara* (line 13) and was resisting like one who did not wish to win the struggle (line 15) may support the insincerity of her resistance. On the other hand, it is he who provides these details and observations, so it is his view of events.

3. The plural possessive adjective *nostrōs* (rather than *meōs*) may suggest that Corinna as well as the poet admired the appearance of her uncovered body. The *ambō* ("both") in line 25 also suggests a shared pleasure in the encounter.

SELECTION X-A & B

STUDENT MATERIALS FOR SELECTION X - B MODIFIED (UNEXPURGATED)
Ovid *Amōrēs* I.5.13–26 Modified

READING VOCABULARY

Line 13 **dēripuī** – dē + rapiō>dēripiō, dēripere, dēripuī, dēreptum: snatch, tear, rip off or down (from her shoulders)

rāra – rārus, -a, -um: thin, scanty i.e. filmy, gauzy

nocēbat – noceō, nocēre, nocuī, nocitum: harm, injure (+ dative)

15 **tamquam** – *conj.*: as, just as, just like

16 **aegrē** – *adv.*: with difficulty, barely

prōditiōne – prōditiō, -iōnis, *f.*: betrayal, treason

17 **vēlāmine** – vēlāmen, -minis, *n.*: clothing, garment, veil

nusquam – *adv.*: nowhere

menda – menda, -ae, *f.*: flaw, blemish, fault

19 **umerōs** – umerus, -ī, *m.*: shoulder

lacertōs – lacertus, -ī, *m.*: (upper)arm, i.e. elbow to shoulder

20 **papillārum** – papilla -ae, *f.*: breast

apta – aptus, -a, -um: fit, suitable, handy, ready, useful

21 **plānus** – plānus, -a, -um: flat, level, even

venter – venter, ventris, *m.* belly, tummy, stomach

castīgātō – castīgātus, -a, -um: firm, disciplined, exercised, well-muscled

22 **femur** – femur, femoris, *n.*: thigh

23 **singula** – singulī, -ae, -a: single, one at a time, individual

referō – referō, referre, rettulī, relātum: bring back, renew, repeat, announce, report, relate, tell

25 **cētera** – cēterus, -a, -um: the other, remaining, rest (of)

lassī – lassus, -a, -um: weary, tired, worn-out, spent

requiēvimus – requiēscō, requiēscere, requiēvī, requiētum: begin to rest up, recover

ambō – ambō, ambae, ambō: both, the two

READING HELPS

Line 13 The significance of the prepositional prefix of *dēripuī* becomes apparent in lines 18–22.

The idea of *multum . . . nocēbat* is close to "nor was it doing much harm;" i.e. it wasn't concealing much because of its fish-net composition.

14 The idea of *tegī pugnābat* approximates "she was struggling to be covered." Note that the infinitive is used here to express purpose. cf. SELECTION VII, Reading Help 4.

15 The opening *quae* is a "connecting" relative and equivalent to *et ea*.

The rather awkward *ita . . . tamquam quae . . .* may be rendered "in such a way (or as if) she . . ." or "like a woman who . . ."

17 Be sure to note the mood of *stetit*. The indicative indicates that *ut* means "as, when" rather than "that, in order that" as with the subjunctive.

pōnō in poetry often has the idea of *dēpōnō*, to put down, lay aside.

19 The *quōs* and *quālēs* are exclamatory: "What . . . what sort of . . ." The exclamations continue in the *qu-* words through line 22.

21 Note the ELLIPSIS in this line.

25 A *-scō* suffix on a verb like *requiēscō* adds the idea of inception: "I begin to rest."

26 Note the independent "jussive" subjunctive construction of *prōveniant*: "let them/may they come forth, turn out or happen."

FYI

Line 2 SYNECDOCHE is a poetic device by which a part stands for, or represents, a whole, so decide what this line *mediō . . . torō* tells the reader about the poem's dramatic situation. When the arrangement of words also pictures the meaning of these words, the poetic technique is called FRAMING. Here is a well-known example from Vergil's *Aeneid*:

Hīc vastō rex Aeolus antrō sedet. "Here king Aeolus sits in a vast cave," where king Aeolus is visually seen within the *vastō . . . antrō*.

ANALYSIS AND COMPREHENSION OF THE LATIN TEXT

1. Concerning line 3's ELLIPSIS, what words are to be inferred from the first half of the line?
2. List the eight participles in the poem and identify the usage of each. Note that *adaperta* and *clausa* with *est* constitute normal passive voice compound verb forms.
3. Note line 2's CHIASTIC word arrangement: ABBA. In this example, note the word picture portrayed: i.e. what are in the middle of the narrow Roman bed?
4. In lines 1–12, which words form an ALLITERATION? a METONYMY? a CHIASMUS? a SYNCHESIS?
5. Consider line 9: what sort of *tunica* would Corinna likely be wearing for this visit?
6. What is the significance of the plural forms *thalamōs* and *multīs . . . virīs* in lines 11–12?
7. In lines 13–26, which words form an HYPERBOLE? a LITOTES? an ANAPHORA?
8. Is the *cum* clause in line 15 expressing circumstance, cause or concession?
9. What type of questions are *Singula quid referam?* and *Cētera quis nescit?* cf. SELECTION VI, Analysis and Comprehension of the Latin Text, 4.

LITERARY ANALYSIS AND DISCUSSION

1. Line 10 discusses Corinna's hairstyle. What are its implications? What nationality do you think she is? From what social background?
2. Some readers interpret line 14's phrase *tegī pugnābat* as Corinna putting on a "show of modesty." Is there evidence in the poem to support this view?
3. In view of all the 1st person, singular verb forms in the poem, what may be the significance of the plural possessive adjective *nostrōs* (rather than *meōs*)?

SELECTION X-A & B

RAPID REVIEW #11
SYNOPSES DRILL

īmus	vultis	ferunt	nōlō	māvīs	fit
ībāmus	volēbātis	ferēbant	nōlēbam	mālēbās	fīēbat
ībimus	volētis	ferent	nōlam	mālēs	fīet
īvimus/iimus	voluistis	tulērunt	nōluī	māluistī	
īverāmus/ierāmus	voluerātis	tulerant	nōlueram	māluerās	
īverimus/ierimus	volueritis	tulerint	nōluerō	malueris	

---

eāmus	velītis	ferant	nōlim	mālīs	fīat
īrēmus	vellētis	ferrent	nollem	mallēs	fieret
īverīmus/ierīmus	voluerītis	tulerint	nōluerim	māluerīs	
īvissēmus/iissēmus	voluissētis	tulissent	nōluissem	māluissēs	

feruntur
ferēbantur
ferentur
lātī, -ae, -a sunt
lātī, -ae, -a erant
<u>lātī, -ae, -a erunt</u>
ferantur
ferrentur
lātī, -ae, -a sint
lātī, -ae, -a essent

CONTEXTUAL SENTENCES

1. My woman prefers to marry no one before me.
2. Suns are able to set and return.
3. Who will approach you now?
4. Has old Love returned?
5. Beautiful/shapely Semiramis is said to have gone into bedrooms.

RAPID REVIEW #12
PRACTICE

asperē	asperius	asperrimē
beātē	beātius	beātissimē
bene	melius	optimē
breviter	brevius	brevissimē
facile*	facilius	facillimē
grātē	grātius	grātissimē
miserē	miserius	miserrimē
mōbiliter	mōbilius	mōbilissimē
nigrē	nigrius	nigerrimē
parum/parvum	minus	minimē
pulchrē	pulchrius	pulcherrimē
similiter	similius	simillimē

*The positive adverb *facile* is a bit irregular, one of a few examples of the adverbial accusative singular. cf. *multum* and *parum* as well. See Bennett, 77 for additional irregularities.

CONTEXTUAL SENTENCES

1. Leisure before (has) destroyed both kings and blessed cities.
2. As soon as Catullus saw (had seen) Lesbia, his tongue quickly grew sluggish (swelled) and a thin flame slowly flowed down beneath his joints.
3. Greetings (Hi there), girlfriend of the Formian, girl with neither a dry mouth and surely not an elegant tongue.
4. Give me a thousand kisses—as quickly as possible!
5. How often the suns shone truly white-hot for you!
6. As long as you burned more greatly not for another (woman), I flourished more brightly (famously) than the Roman Ilia.
7. What woman did the poet used to love very much?
8. May mid-days like this come about for me more often!
9. Chloe was trembling very greatly both in heart and in knees.
10. Catullus thought that the poem had been charmingly begun by his friend.

SELECTION XI – A & B

TRANSLATION

    Every lover is a soldier, and Cupid has his own camp;
        Atticus, believe me, every lover is a soldier.
    The time of life, which is suitable for war, suits Venus also.
        A disgraceful thing is an old soldier, a disgraceful thing is an old man's love.
5   The courage which a general sought in a brave soldier,
        this a pretty girl seeks in her male companion:
    both are on guard all night, each begins to rest on the ground;
        that one guards his mistress' door, but that one his general's.
    The soldier's task is a long road: dispatch a girl,
10   the vigorous lover will follow with border taken away;
    he'll go into obstructing mountains and streams doubled by a cloudburst,
        that man will trample over piled up snow,
    and when he is about to be atop straits he will not plead as excuse the swell-causing
        winds of Eurus or ask for weather suitable for skimming over the waters.
15   Who except either a soldier or lover will endure both the chills of the night
        and snow mixed with heavy hail?
    One is sent as a spy on deadly enemies,
        the other keeps his eyes on a rival, as on a foe.
    That one lays siege to important cities, this one to the threshold of a hard girlfriend;
20   the one breaks gates, but the other, doors.
    Often it has been useful to attack the enemy buried in sleep
        and to slay the unarmed throng with an armed band.
    Thus the fierce columns of Thracian Rhesus fell,
        and you, O captured horses, deserted your master.
25   Without a doubt lovers employ the sleep times of husbands
        and move their weapons when the enemy has been put to sleep.
    It is necessary for the soldier and the wretched lover
        to go past bands of guards and squads of sentinels.
    Mars is uncertain, nor is Venus sure: the overcome rise again
30   and those whom you would deny ever to be able to go down, fall.
    Therefore, whoever was calling love laziness
        should cease: Love is something of an active character.

Mīlitat omnis amāns, et Cupīdō sua castra habet;
　　Attice, crēde mihi, mīlitat omnis amāns.
Aetās, quae bellō est habilis, Venerī quoque convenit.
　　Turpe senex mīles, turpe senīlis amor.
5　Quōs animōs ducēs petiēre in mīlite fortī,
　　hōs bella puella petit in sociō virō:
pervigilant ambō, terrā requiescit uterque;
　　ille forēs dominae servat, at ille ducis.
Mīlitis officium longa est via: mitte puellam,
10　　strenuus amāns fīne exemptō sequētur;
ībit in adversōs montēs duplicātaque nimbō
　　flūmina, ille congestās exteret nivēs,
nec freta pressūrus tumidōs causābitur Eurōs
　　aut sīdera quaeret apta verrendīs aquīs.
15　Quis nisi vel mīles vel amāns et frīgora noctis
　　et nivēs densō imbre mixtās perferet?
Mittitur speculātor alter infestōs in hostēs,
　　in rīvāle, ut hoste, alter tenet oculōs.
Ille gravēs urbēs, hic dūrae līmen amīcae
20　　obsidet; hic portās frangit, at ille forēs.
Saepe sopōrātōs invādere profuit hostēs
　　et caedere armātā vulgus inerme manū.
Sīc fera Thrēiciī cecidērunt agmina Rhēsī,
　　et dominum dēseruistis, captī equī.
25　Nempe marītōrum somnīs ūtuntur amantēs
　　et sua sopītīs hostibus arma movent.
Custōdum transīre manūs vigilumque catervās
　　mīlitis et miserī semper amantis opus.
Mars dubius, nec certa Venus: victīque resurgunt
30　　quōsque negēs umquam posse iacēre, cadunt.
Ergō dēsidiam quīcumque vocābat amōrem,
　　dēsinat: ingeniī est experientis Amor.

ANALYSIS AND COMPREHENSION OF THE LATIN TEXT

1. The antecedent of *sua* is *Cupīdō*. The antecedent of line 8's first *ille* is the lover (*amāns*), of the second it is the soldier (*mīles*). The antecedent of line 12's *ille* is the lover (*amāns*).

2. Verb forms:
   a. *habet* is present active indicative
   b. *crēde* is present active imperative
   c. *convenit* is present active indicative
   d. *sequētur* is deponent future indicative
   e. *exteret* is future active indicative
   f. *quaeret* is future active indicative

3. Six participles and usage:
   a. *amāns* (3x: lines 1, 2 & 10) used as a substantive
   b. *exemptō* in line 10 is used in an Ablative Absolute.
   c. *duplicāta* in line 11 is used as a Regular Adjectival Modifier
   d. *congestās* in line 12 is used as a Regular Adjectival Modifier
   e. *pressūrus* in line 13 is used as a Regular Adjectival Modifier
   f. *verrendīs* in line 14 is used as a Regular Adjectival Modifier (gerund substitute)

4. A similar musical term is **SYNCOPATION**.

5. In his pursuit of the *puellam*, the *strenuus amāns* undertakes:

   to follow (*sequētur*)

   to go to mountains and rivers (*ībit*)

   to trample over snow (*exteret*)

   not to make excuses (*nec . . . causābitur*)

   or to seek smooth sailing (*quaeret*)

6. **ANAPHORA** occurs in line 4's *turpe . . . turpe*. One might take the repeated opening phrase as **ANAPHORA** as well.

7. *Verrendīs aquīs* is dative, for the adjective *apta* patterns with the dative case.

8. **APOSTROPHE** occurs in line 24's *captī equī*.

9. **SYNECDOCHE** occurs in line 19's *līmen* where the threshold of the doorway stands for the whole door. **METONYMY** is employed when the poet used Cupid, Venus and Amor to represent love, Eurus to represent the wind, and Mars to represent war. **CHIASMUS** occurs in line 16's *nivēs . . . mixtās*, in line 22's *armātā . . . manū*, in line 26's *sua . . . arma*, and in line 29's *Mars . . . Venus*. **SYNCHESIS** occurs in line 23's *fera Thrēiciī . . . agmina Rhēsī*, as well as in line 27's *custōdum . . . manūs vigilumque catervās*.

LITERARY ANALYSIS AND DISCUSSION

1. Some readers may find the suggestion hard to accept, thinking that ancient literary figures were unlikely to be so subtle or sophisticated. A discussion of then current principles of artistic composition (Hellenistic Greek's Alexandrian poetry, Catullus and the *poetae novī*, Vergil's subjective style, Horace's mosaic word placement, etc.) may fit in well at this point (the final Selection) and can be enlightening.

2. The poet's conclusion is that love is anything but leisurely idleness (*dēsidiam*); on the contrary, it is marked by activity and planning (*ingeniī . . . experientis*).

SELECTION XI-A & B

RAPID REVIEW #13
PRACTICE

1. | hic puer | haec puella | hoc oppidum |
    |---|---|---|
    | hūius puerī | hūius puellae | hūius oppidī |
    | huic puerō | huic puellae | huic oppidō |
    | hunc puerum | hanc puellam | hoc oppidum |
    | hōc puerō | hāc puellā | hōc oppidō |
    | hī puerī | hae puellae | haec oppida |
    | hōrum puerōrum | hārum puellārum | hōrum oppidōrum |
    | hīs puerīs | hīs puellīs | hīs oppidīs |
    | hōs puerōs | hās puellās | haec oppida |
    | hīs puerīs | hīs puellīs | hīs oppidīs |

2. | ille rex | illa lex | illud mare |
    |---|---|---|
    | illīus rēgis | illīus lēgis | illīus maris |
    | illī rēgī | illī lēgī | illī marī |
    | illum rēgem | illam lēgem | illud mare |
    | illō rēge | illā lēge | illō marī |
    | illī rēgēs | illae lēgēs | illa maria |
    | illōrum rēgum | illārum lēgum | illōrum marium |
    | illīs rēgibus | illīs lēgibus | illīs maribus |
    | illōs rēgēs | illās lēgēs | illa maria |
    | illīs rēgibus | illīs lēgibus | illīs maribus |

3. | is exercitus | ea rēs | id cornū |
    |---|---|---|
    | eius exercitūs | eius reī | eius cornūs |
    | eī exercituī | eī reī | eī cornū |
    | eum exercitum | eam rem | id cornū |
    | eō exercitū | eā rē | eō cornū |
    | eī exercitūs | eae rēs | ea cornua |
    | eōrum exercituum | eārum rērum | eōrum cornuum |
    | eīs exercitibus | eīs rēbus | eīs cornibus |
    | eōs exercitūs | eās rēs | ea cornua |
    | eīs exercitibus | eīs rēbus | eīs cornibus |

CONTEXTUAL SENTENCES

1. That one (He) seems to me to be equal to a god, ...
2. These things I admit/grant one-by-one/individually in this way.
3. Although that one (he) is more handsome than a star, you more fickle than a cork, ...
4. Now this wall will have my weapons ...
5. That light must be provided for shy/modest girls.
6. But that one (she) was struggling to be covered by her tunic.
7. A beautiful girl seeks these spirits/this courage in a male partner.
8. That man (He) guards the door of his mistress, but that one (he) that of his general.
9. That lover will trample upon heaped up snow.
10. That man (The former) lays siege to important cities, this man (the latter) to the threshold of his hard (hearted) girlfriend.

UNIT REVIEW ANSWER KEY

CATULLUS 51 Unmodified

Ille mī pār esse deō vidētur,
ille, sī fās est, superāre dīvōs,
quī sedēns adversus identidem tē
    spectat et audit

5   dulce rīdentem, miserō quod omnēs
ēripit sensūs mihi: nam simul tē,
Lesbia, aspexī, nihil est super mī
    [vōcis in ōre]

lingua sed torpet, tenuis sub artūs
10   flamma dēmānat, sonitū suōpte
tintinant aurēs, geminā teguntur
    lūmina nocte.

Ōtium, Catulle, tibi molestum est;
ōtiō exsultās nimiumque gestīs.
15   Ōtium et regēs prius et beātās
    perdidit urbēs.

CATULLUS 51 Unmodified. Meter: Sapphic Stanza

```
— ⌣ | — — | — ⌣ ⌣ | — ⌣ | — ×
```
Ille mī pār esse deō vidētur,
```
— ⌣ | — — | — ‖ ⌣ ⌣ | — ⌣ | — ×
```
ille, sī fās est, superāre dīvōs,
```
— ⌣ | — — | — ⌣ ⌣ | — ⌣ | — ×
```
quī sedēns adversus identidem tē
```
— ⌣ ⌣ | — ×
```
spectat et audit

```
— ⌣ | — — | — ‖ ⌣ ⌣ | — ⌣ | — ×
```
5 dulce rīdentem, miserō quod omnēs
```
— ⌣ | — — | — ‖ ⌣ ⌣ | — ⌣ | — ×
```
ēripit sensūs mihi: nam simul tē,
```
— ⌣ | — — | — ‖ ⌣ ⌣ | — ⌣ | — ×
```
Lesbi(a), aspexī, nihil est super mī
```
— ⌣ ⌣ | — ×
```
[vōcis in ōre]

```
— ⌣ | — — | — ‖ ⌣ ⌣ | — ⌣ | — ×
```
lingua sed torpet, tenuis sub artūs
```
— ⌣ | — — | — ‖ ⌣ ⌣ | — ⌣ | — ×
```
10 flamma dēmānat, sonitū suōpte
```
— ⌣ | — — | — ‖ ⌣ ⌣ | — ⌣ | — ×
```
tintinant aurēs, gemināphone teguntur
```
— ⌣ ⌣ | — ×
```
lūmina nocte.

```
— ⌣ | — — ⌣ | — ⌣ ‖ ⌣ | — ⌣ | — ×
```
Ōtium, Catulle[1], tibi molestum (e)st;
```
— ⌣ | — — | — ‖ ⌣ ⌣ | — ⌣ | — ×
```
ōti(ō) exsultās nimiumque gestīs.
```
— ⌣ | — — ⌣ | — ‖ ⌣ ⌣ | — ⌣ | — ×
```
15 Ōti(um) et regēs prius et beātās
```
— ⌣ ⌣ | — ×
```
perdidit urbēs.

---

[1] The fourth syllable in lines 1-3 of each stanza is sometimes short (as in lines 13 and 15).

TRANSLATION

    That man to me seems to be equal to a god,
    he, if it is right, to surpass the gods,
    who, sitting opposite, again and again
        looks at you and hears you

5   laughing sweetly, which snatches away
    all senses for (from) wretched me: for as soon as
    I have looked at you, Lesbia, for me no voice
        is left over in my mouth

    but my tongue is numb, beneath my joints
10   a thin flame spreads, with their own sound
    my ears ring, and my eyes are covered
        by twin night.

    "Doing your own thing," Catullus, for you is an annoyance:
    in "doing your own thing" you exult and you overly desire it.
15   "Doing one's own thing" earlier destroyed both kings
        and blessed cities.

UNIT REVIEW ANSWER KEY

POINTS TO PONDER
Cat. 51

1. The *ille* may be "god-like" in his enjoyment of Lesbia's company, a "blessing" of such a unique nature that it elevates him to the ranks of the divine. Such a reading implicitly suggests that Lesbia is a goddess in her attractiveness and charm. By such a suggestion the poet flatters and praises Lesbia's beauty so as to gain her positive attention.

    John Ferguson suggests a more **IRONIC**, tongue-in-cheek reading of the description of the man as "god-like." He interprets the description to mean that the man has to have divine strength and staying power to keep up with and satisfy Lesbia physically. Such a reading assumes that her lusty appetites and dominating nature were already known to the poet. It also suggests that the poem is not the first of the Lesbia poems but that the poet had already met her and found in her a bossy and demanding lover.

2. Agreement with Small's assessment would be based on the poet's apparent jealousy of *ille* and on the apparent physical ill-effects described in lines 6–12. Disagreement with Small's assessment would read the physical effects as indications of the poet's infatuation and youthful inexperience. The poem thus is filled with **HYPERBOLE** – and ambiguity.

3. If the stanza was added after the affair ended, it might suggest the priority of reason over passion as the poet, addressing himself, reminds himself of the possible cost of such passion. In such a reading, the poet reflects upon a life of *otium* that permitted such a state of affairs.

    Agreement with the assessment may indicate Catullus' frustration with *otium*: his life of leisure allows him too much time to <u>obsess</u> about Lesbia and/or her possible lovers. Disagreement with the assessment may hold that leisure is an escape, a freedom akin to oblivion.

    If "kings" and whole "cities" were ruined (*perdidit*) on account of *otium*, surely an ordinary individual must be on guard lest (s)he too fall prey to its appeal. Alternatively, the words could also continue the **HYPERBOLE**, not being meant to be taken seriously, and hence be considered irrelevant.

4. Most interpreters of Catullan poetry see the poem as addressed not to the unnamed *ille* but primarily to Lesbia and to Catullus himself, and ultimately – like any poem – to the reading audience.

CATULLUS 43 Unmodified

Salvē, nec minimō puella nāsō
nec bellō pede nec nigrīs ocellīs
nec longīs digitīs nec ōre siccō
nec sānē nimis ēlegante linguā,
5   dēcoctōris amīca Formiānī.
Tēn Prōvincia narrat esse bellam?
Tēcum Lesbia nostra comparātur?
Ō saeclum insapiēns et infacētum!

CATULLUS 43 Unmodified. Meter: Hendecasyllables

```
— —| —   ᴗ ᴗ| —   ᴗ|—ᴗ |— ×
```
Salvē, nec minimō puella nāsō
```
— —|—   ᴗ ᴗ|—   ᴗ|— ᴗ|— ×
```
nec bellō pede nec nigrīs ocellīs
```
— —|—   ᴗ ᴗ|—   ᴗ|—ᴗ|— ×
```
nec longīs digitīs nec ōre siccō
```
— —|—   ᴗ  ᴗ|—ᴗ|—  ᴗ| —  ×
```
nec sānē nimis ēlegante linguā,
```
— —|—ᴗ   ᴗ|—ᴗ | —  ᴗ|—×
```
5   dēcoctōris amīca Formiānī.
```
—   —|—   ᴗᴗ| —  ᴗ|—   ᴗ |— ×
```
Tēn Prōvincia narrat esse bellam?
```
— — | —   ᴗᴗ| —   ᴗ| —   ᴗ|— ×
```
Tēcum Lesbia nostra comparātur?
```
— — |   —   ᴗ ᴗ|—   ᴗ |— ᴗ|— ×
```
Ō saecl(um) insapiēns et infacētum!

TRANSLATION

    Hi there, girl, not very small-nosed
    nor pretty-footed nor dark-eyed
    nor long-fingered nor dry-mouthed
    nor, surely!, too elegant-tongued,
5   girlfriend of the bankrupt guy from Formiae.
    The province says YOU are pretty?
    With YOU our (my) Lesbia is compared?
    Oh, a tasteless and witless generation!

POINTS TO PONDER
Cat. 43

1. Most readers find the *salvē* sarcastic, noting that the rest of the poem is anything but friendly or complimentary to the *amīca*.

2. The poet gains a heightened contrast between the unattractive, unrefined friend of Mamurra and Lesbia who by implication has real beauty in <u>all</u> areas.

3. Line 5 offers a word picture of the *amīca* embraced (surrounded, enfolded) by her lover, the *dēcoctōris . . . Formiānī*.

4. While it is possible that Catullus was mocking provincial standards from his urban position, it is also true that Mamurra's power and influence in the provinces made it politically discreet for anyone living there to describe his *amīca* as *bella*.

CATULLUS 86 Unmodified

Quintia formōsa est multīs; mihi candida, longa,
    recta est. Haec ego sīc singula confiteor,
tōtum illud formōsa negō: nam nulla venustās,
    nulla in tam magnō est corpore mīca salis.
5 Lesbia formōsa est, quae cum pulcherrima tōta est,
    tum omnibus ūna omnēs surripuit Venerēs.

CATULLUS 86 Unmodified. Meter: Elegiac couplet

— ⏑⏑| — —| —   —| ⏑ ⏑ |— ⏑ ⏑ | — ×
Quintia formōsa (e)st multīs; mihi candida, longa,
— — | — ⏑ ⏑ |— ‖— ⏑ ⏑ |— ⏑ ⏑|×
recta (e)st. Haec ego sīc singula confiteor,
—   — |—   —|— ⏑ ⏑ |— —| — ⏑ ⏑|— ×
tōt(um) illud formōsa negō: nam nulla venustās,
—   — | —   —| —   ‖— ⏑ ⏑|— ⏑ ⏑| ×
null(a) in tam magnō (e)st corpore mīca salis.
5 — ⏑⏑| — — |—   — |—   — | — ⏑ ⏑|— ×
Lesbia formōsa (e)st, quae cum pulcherrima tōta (e)st,
—   ⏑ ⏑| —   —| — ‖— ⏑ ⏑ |— ⏑ ⏑| ×
t(um) omnibus ūn(a) omnēs surripuit Venerēs.

TRANSLATION

    Quintia is beautiful to many; to me she is fair-skinned, tall,
        and has a good posture: I grant these things individually like this.
    I deny that <u>that</u> totality is beautiful: for there is not any charm,
        not any grain of wit (spark of taste) in so great a body.
5   Lesbia is beautiful, who is both very pretty as a whole
        And from all all by herself has stolen all the Venuses (charms of Venus).

POINTS TO PONDER
Cat. 86

1. Students generally are quick to notice several contrasts such as: *multīs/mihi; singula/tōtum; confiteor/negō; omnibus/ūna/omnēs* (there are others as well). Word order, e.g. the parallelism of *Quintia* and *Lesbia* and the juxtaposition of *multīs/mihi*, emphasizes these contrasts.

2. The contrast in size and idea between *magnō corpore* and *mīca salis* provides humor.

3. Most readers do not see *formōsa* and *pulcherrima* as having parallel meanings, sensing that the former is almost exclusively physical (shapely, attractively figured) while the latter includes wit (*salis*) and charm/grace (*venustās*) as well. The *cum . . . tum* correlative pairing associates *venustās* clearly and powerfully with *pulcherrima*.

CATULLUS 5 Unmodified

Vīvāmus, mea Lesbia, atque amēmus,
rūmōrēsque senum sevēriōrum
omnēs ūnius aestimēmus assis!
Sōlēs occidere et redīre possunt:
5   nōbīs cum semel occidit brevis lux,
nox est perpetua ūna dormienda.
Da mī bāsia mille, deinde centum,
dein mille altera, dein secunda centum,
deinde usque altera mille, deinde centum.
10 Dein, cum mīlia multa fēcerīmus,
conturbābimus illa, nē sciāmus,
aut nē quis malus invidēre possit,
cum tantum sciat esse bāsiōrum.

CATULLUS 5 Unmodified. Meter: Hendecasyllables

```
— — | —   ᴗᴗ | —   ᴗ | —    ᴗ | — ×
```
Vīvāmus, mea Lesbi(a), atqu(e) amēmus,
```
—   — | —   ᴗ   ᴗ | —   ᴗ | —  ᴗ | — ×
```
rūmōrēsque senum sevēriōrum
```
—   — | — ᴗᴗ | —   ᴗ | —   ᴗ | — ×
```
omnēs ūnius¹ aestimēmus assis!
```
—  — | —   ᴗ   ᴗ | —   ᴗ | — ᴗ | —   ×
```
Sōlēs occider(e) et redīre possunt:

5
```
—   — | —   ᴗ   ᴗ | — ᴗ | — ᴗ | —   ×
```
nōbīs cum semel occidit brevis lux,
```
—   — | —   ᴗ ᴗ | —  ᴗ | —  ᴗ | — ×
```
nox est perpetu(a) ūna dormienda.
```
ᴗ  — | —  ᴗᴗ | —   ᴗ | —    ᴗ | —  ×
```
Da mī bāsia mille, deinde centum,
```
—   — |  —   ᴗ  ᴗ | —   ᴗ | — ᴗ | — ×
```
dein mill(e) altera, dein secunda centum,
```
—    — | —   ᴗ  ᴗ | —   ᴗ | —   ᴗ | — ×
```
deind(e) usqu(e) altera mille, deinde centum.

10
```
—    — | — ᴗᴗ | —   ᴗ | — ᴗ | — ×
```
Dein, cum mīlia multa fēcerīmus²,
```
—   — | — ᴗ  ᴗ | —  ᴗ | —  ᴗ | — ×
```
conturbābimus illa, nē sciāmus,
```
—    —| —   ᴗ ᴗ | — ᴗ | — ᴗ | —   ×
```
aut nē quis malus invidēre possit,
```
—    — | —   ᴗ ᴗ | — ᴗ | — ᴗ | — ×
```
cum tantum sciat esse bāsiōrum.

---

¹ Catullus is inconsistent in his treatment of the –i- in *ūnius*. Here it is a "short" –i, as the scansion indicates.

² Daniel Garrison, *ad loc.*, points out that "the future perfect indicative with a long –ī, normal in Cicero, occurs here in verse for the first time.

TRANSLATION

      Let us live, my Lesbia, and let us love,
      And let us rate the rumors – all of them –
      of the too strict old men as worth an *as*.
      Suns are able to go down and return:
5   (but) for us when once and for all the brief light has gone down,
      one eternal night must be slept.
      Give me a thousand kisses, then a hundred,
      then a second thousand, than a following hundred,
      then all the way to another thousand, then a hundred.
10   Then, since we have made many thousands,
      We'll thoroughly mix them all up, lest we know,
      Or lest any evil man be able to be jealous of/to bewitch us
      Since he knows that there is so much of kisses (are so many kisses).

POINTS TO PONDER
Cat. 5

1. The word order of line 1 pictures how *mea Lesbia* is the center of the poet's love-life in which the two are joined.

2. Other instances of tight artistic control may include:

    a. The balance of two infinitives *occidere* and *redīre* to two verbs *vīvāmus . . . atque amēmus* with the contrast between the sun's ongoing movement and death's immobility.

    b. The careful lessening from 3 to 2 to 1 syllable in *occidit brevis lux*.

    c. The careful contrast between *omnēs* and *ūnius* as well as *lux* and *nox*.

    d. Three monosyllabic words *lux, nox* and *est* followed by the polysyllabic *perpetua* elided into *ūna* to lengthen death's sleep still more.

3. After a call to love (theme 1) in lines 1–3 and the rationale of death's approaching finality (theme 2) in lines 4-6, the *carpe diem* theme in lines 7–9 suggests the ecstasy of the poet's unbridled and uncontrollable passion. The **ANAPHORA** of *dein . . . deinde . . . deinde . . . dein* reinforces the idea of piling up the kisses.

4. Some instances of superstitiousness include the multiples of the number 3, the attempt to obtain uncertainty as to the precise number of kisses, and the attempt to avoid the "evil eye."

CATULLUS 70 Unmodified

Nullī sē dīcit mulier mea nūbere malle
 quam mihi, nōn sī sē Iuppiter ipse petat.
Dīcit: sed mulier cupidō quod dīcit amantī
 in ventō et rapidā scrībere oportet aquā.

CATULLUS 70 Unmodified. Meter: Elegiac Couplet

```
—  —|—  —|—    ⌣ ⌣|—   ⌣⌣ |—  ⌣ ⌣ |—   ×
```
Nullī sē dīcit mulier mea nūbere malle
```
—     ⌣ ⌣ | —   —|—‖—    ⌣ ⌣ |—  ⌣  ⌣ |×
```
quam mihi, nōn sī sē Iuppiter ipse petat.
```
——  |—     ⌣ ⌣|—  ⌣ ⌣|—    —  |—  ⌣ ⌣| — ×
```
Dīcit: sed mulier cupidō quod dīcit amantī
```
—   —|  —    ⌣ ⌣|—‖  — ⌣    ⌣ | —  ⌣  ⌣| ×
```
in vent(ō) et rapidā scrīber(e) oportet aquā.

TRANSLATION

My woman says that she prefers to marry none
    before me, not if Jupiter himself should seek her.
She says this: but whatever a woman says to a desirous lover
    one should write on the wind and rapid water.

POINTS TO PONDER
Cat. 70

1. Catullus' usage of *mulier* in this poem may imply a lowered estimation of her in light of his discovery that her promises lack substance. He may be expressing his disappointment, frustration, disenchantment or anger.

2. The lack of a *mea* with *mulier* in line 3 indicates the more generalized idea – what a woman says to a lover (instead of what my (*mea*) woman says to me (*mihi*)).

   The *mulier* of line 3 is not the *mulier* of line 1 (who was Lesbia), and consequently refers to generalized "Woman."

   In similar fashion, the *amantī* of line 3 is not the *mihi* of line 2, but a generalized "Lover."

3. Though metrics are not emphasized in the *Libellus*, this may be an appropriate occasion to point out how the elision between *ventō* and *et* emphasizes the impermanence of the two separate nouns (wind and water). Furthermore, the numerous dactyls by their quickness highlight the impermanence.

4. The poet stresses the importance of *dīcit* by a triple **ANAPHORA**.

   Something written is generally considered more permanent than something said, but when written on wind or wave the expected permanence is cleverly undercut all the more strongly.

5. The poet's mood as he describes his distrust is restrained, for he does not openly reproach her so much as excuse the unreliability. He notes that such behavior is a generic trait of womankind, not just of Lesbia. Though a stereotype, some readers see it as an almost affectionately indulgent reaction, though he does openly state his disbelief in her words.

CATULLUS 8 Unmodified

Miser Catulle, dēsinās ineptīre,
et quod vidēs perīsse perditum dūcās.
Fulsēre quondam candidī tibi sōlēs,
cum ventitābās quō puella dūcēbat
5 amāta nōbīs quantum amābitur nulla.
Ibi illa multa tum iocōsa fīēbant,
quae tū volēbās nec puella nōlēbat.
Fulsēre vērē candidī tibi sōlēs.
Nunc iam illa nōn volt: tū quoque impotēns [nōlī],
10 nec quae fugit sectāre, nec miser vīve,
<u>sed obstinātā mente perfer, obdūrā.</u>

Valē, puella. Iam Catullus obdūrat,
nec tē requīret nec rogābit invītam:
at tū dolēbis, cum rogāberis nulla.
15 Scelesta, vae tē. Quae tibi manet vīta?
Quis nunc tē adībit? Cui vidēberis bella?
Quem nunc amābis? Cūius esse dīcēris?
Quem bāsiābis? Cui labella mordēbis?
At tū, Catulle, dēstinātus obdūrā.

CATULLUS 8 Unmodified. Meter: Choliambic (Limping Iambic, Scazon)

⏑ — | ⏑ — |⏑ — |⏑ — | ⏑ — |— ×
Miser Catulle, dēsinās ineptīre,

— — | ⏑ — | ⏑ —|⏑ — |⏑ — | — ×
et quod vidēs perīsse perditum dūcās.

— —|⏑ — | — — | ⏑—|⏑—| — ×
Fulsēre quondam candidī tibi¹ sōlēs,

— — |⏑ —|— — | ⏑ —|⏑ —|— ×
cum ventitābās quō puella dūcēbat

⏑ —|⏑ —|— — | ⏑ —| ⏑— | — ×
5 **amāta nōbīs quant(um) amābitur nulla.**

⏑ — |⏑ — |⏑ — |⏑ — |⏑ —|— ×
Ib(i) illa multa tum iocōsa fīēbant,

— —| ⏑ —|— — | ⏑—|⏑ —|— ×
quae tū volēbās nec puella nōlēbat.

— —|⏑ —|— —| ⏑—| ⏑—| — ×
Fulsēre vērē candidī tibi sōlēs.

— — |⏑ — |— —| ⏑ —| ⏑ — | — ×
Nunc i(am) illa nōn volt: tū quoqu(e) impotēns [nōlī],

— — | ⏑ — |— —|⏑ — | ⏑ —|— ×
10 **nec quae fugit sectāre, nec miser vīve,**

⏑ —| ⏑—|— — | ⏑ — |⏑ — |— ×
<u>**sed obstinātā mente perfer, obdūrā.**</u>

⏑ — | ⏑ —|⏑ — | ⏑ —|⏑ — | —×
Valē, puella. Iam Catullus obdūrat,

— —|⏑ —|— — | ⏑ — |⏑ —|— ×
nec tē requīret nec rogābit invītam:

— —|⏑ —|— — | ⏑ —|⏑ —| — ×
at tū dolēbis, cum rogāberis nulla.

⏑ —|⏑ — |— — | —|⏑— | ⏑ — |— ×
15 **Scelesta, vae tē. Quae tibi manet vīta?**

— — | ⏑ —|— —| ⏑ — |⏑ —|— ×
Quis nunc t(ē) adībit? Cui vidēberis bella?

— — |⏑ — |— —|⏑ —|⏑ —|—×
Quem nunc amābis? Cūius esse dīcēris?

— —|⏑—|— — | ⏑—|⏑ — | — ×
Quem bāsiābis? Cui labella mordēbis?

— — | ⏑ — |⏑ — |⏑ —|⏑ —|— ×
At tū, Catulle, dēstinātus obdūrā.

---

¹ Catullus is inconsistent in his treatment of the final -i in *tibi* (and *mihi*). Here, and in lines 8 and 15, it scans as a "long" -ī.

TRANSLATION

      Miserable Catullus, you should stop being a fool,
      and that which you see to have perished you should consider destroyed.
      Formerly suns shone bright for you,
      when you always used to come where the girl was leading,
5   loved by us as much as not any will be loved.
      Then, when those many jolly times used to happen
      which you were wanting nor was that girl not wanting,
      suns shone truly bright for you.
      Now that girl no longer is willing; you too, powerless one, be unwilling,
10   and do not keep following after one who flees, and do not live miserable,
      <u>but stick it out with resolute mind, be firm.</u>

      Goodbye, girl! Now Catullus is firm,
      he will not ask you back nor will he ask you unwilling:
      but you'll be sad, when you will be asked not at all.
15   Wicked woman, damn you! What life remains for you?
      Who now will visit you? To whom will you seem lovely?
      Whom now will you love? Whose will you be said to be?
      Whom will you kiss? Whose little lips will you nibble?
      But you, Catullus, having made up your mind, be firm.

POINTS TO PONDER
Cat. 8

1. Catullus obviously names himself in this poem of self-address. Yet one may also wonder if he names only himself and not his lover because he finds it too painful to mention her by name.

   The absence of the usual *mea* with *puella* highlights that the affair has been broken off, and so she is no longer <u>his</u> *puella*.

2. Ferguson points out three things gained by this technique:

   a. It gives the reader some detachment from a very self-centered poem, adding objectivity to a very subjective work of art.

   b. It makes it easier for the poet to use a light, conversational tone with simple and direct language.

   c. It makes possible emotional movement that increases the effectiveness of the poem that is arranged around three commands to endure: lines 1–2, lines 9–11 and line 19.

3. The authors' students generally have found Garrison's suggestion more appropriate due to the poet's self-pity (*miser Catullus*) over his rejection by her. Forsyth's "unlucky" and Lyne's "unfortunate" were, in their view, too sympathetic to the woman. From the poet's viewpoint, he, not she, deserves sympathy.

4. The change from polite command to forceful imperative may result from Catullus' emotional upset and inability to achieve the rational perspective he urges upon himself. The reader notes a deterioration from coolly rational self-control to heated emotionality.

HORACE *Odes* I.23 Unmodified

Vītās innuleō mē similis, Chloē,
quaerentī pavidam montibus āviīs
    matrem nōn sine vānō
        aurārum et silvae metū.

5   Nam seu mōbilibus vēris inhorruit
adventus foliīs, seu viridēs rubum
    dīmōvēre lacertae,
        et corde et genibus tremit.

Atquī nōn ego tē tigris ut aspera
10   Gaetūlusve leō frangere persequor:
    tandem dēsine matrem
        tempestīva sequī virō.

HORACE *Odes* I.23 Unmodified
Meter: Fourth Asclepiadean Stanza

$$— — | — \cup \cup — \| — \cup \cup | — \cup \times$$
Vītās innuleō mē similis, Chloē,
$$— — | — \cup \cup — \| — \cup \cup | — \cup \times$$
quaerentī pavidam montibus āviīs
$$— — | — \cup \cup | — \cup \times$$
matrem nōn sine vānō
$$— — | — \cup \cup | — \cup \times$$
aurār(um) et silvae[1] metū.

5
$$— — | — \cup \cup — \| — \cup \cup | — \cup \times$$
Nam seu mōbilibus vēris inhorruit
$$— — | — \cup \cup — \| — \cup \cup | — \cup \times$$
adventus foliīs, seu viridēs rubum
$$— — | — \cup \cup | — \cup \times$$
dīmōvēre lacertae,
$$— — | — \cup \cup | — \cup \times$$
et cord(e) et genibus tremit.

$$— — | — \cup \cup — \| — \cup \cup | — \cup \times$$
Atquī nōn ego tē tigris ut aspera
$$— — | — \cup \cup — \| — \cup \cup | — \cup \times$$
10   Gaetūlusve leō frangere persequor:
$$— — | — \cup \cup | — \cup \times$$
tandem dēsine matrem
$$— — | — \cup \cup | — \cup \times$$
tempestīva sequī virō.

---

[1] *Silvae* is sometimes written as *siluae* and treated, as here, as a three-syllable word. Hence the syllabification and scansion are *si-lu-ae*.

TRANSLATION

      You avoid me like a fawn, Chloe,
      seeking her quaking mother on pathless mountains
          not without a vain
              fear of the breezes and forest.

5   For whether the arrival of spring has rustled
      in the moving leaves or green lizards
          have moved apart the bramble,
              she trembles both in heart and knees.

      But I do not pursue you like a fierce tigress
10   or Gaetulian lion to break you:
          finally stop following your mother,
              ripe for a man.

POINTS TO PONDER
Hor. *Odes* I. 23

1. The fact that the fawn's mother is described as *pavidam* suggests that Chloe has been raised by a protective (overly?) mother whose daughter has now strayed out of her sight in unfamiliar surroundings and may not be able to find her way back. An overly protected offspring may lack self-confidence.

2. The poet in the last stanza asserts that there is no need for her to fear him, since he is not after her like a tigress or lion to do her harm. He also asserts that she is ready/ripe for a man and should stop following her mother.

3. The connection between the imagery and the phrase *tempesīva . . . virō* may lie in seeing that the imagery presents a **METAPHOR** for a girl's first sexual experience with a male. Rather than apologizing for this reality, the poet encourages Chloe to accept the facts of her situation. She is now *tempestīva virō*.

HORACE *Odes* III. 9 Unmodified

"Dōnec grātus eram tibi
   nec quisquam potior bracchia candidae
cervīcī iuvenis dabat,
   Persārum viguī rēge beātior."

5   "Dōnec nōn aliā magis
   arsistī neque erat Lȳdia post Chloēn,
multī Lȳdia nōminis
   Rōmānā viguī clārior Īliā."

"Mē nunc Thressa Chloē regit,
10   dulcēs docta modōs et citharae sciēns,
prō quā nōn metuam morī,
   sī parcent animae fāta superstitī."

"Mē torret face mūtuā
   Thūrīnī Calais fīlius Ornytī,
15   prō quō bis patiar morī,
   sī parcent puerō fāta superstitī."

"Quid sī prisca redit Venus
   dīductōsque iugō cōgit aēneō?
Sī flāva excutitur Chloē
20   reiectaeque patet iānua Lȳdiae?"

"Quamquam sīdere pulchrior
   ille est, tū levior cortice et improbō
īrācundior Hadriā,
   tēcum vīvere amem, tēcum obeam libēns!"

HORACE *Odes* III. 9 Unmodified
Meter: Second Asclepiadean Stanza

$$— \ — \ | \ — \ \cup \ \cup \ | — \ \cup \ \times$$
"Dōnec grātus eram tibi
$$— \quad — \ | \ — \quad \cup \ \cup — \| — \quad \cup\cup | — \quad \cup \ \times$$
    nec quisquam potior bracchia candidae
$$— \ —|— \cup \quad \cup \ |— \quad \cup \ \times$$
cervīcī iuvenis dabat,
$$— \ —| — \quad \cup \ \cup —\|— \ \cup \quad \cup|— \ \cup\times$$
    Persārum viguī rēge beātior."

$$— \ — \ | \ — \quad \cup\cup|— \quad \cup \ \times$$
5 "Dōnec nōn aliā magis
$$——|— \ \cup \quad \cup \ —\| — \ \cup\cup \ | \ — \quad \cup \ \times$$
    arsistī nequ(e) erat Lȳdia¹ post Chloēn,
$$— \ —|— \ \cup\cup| \ — \ \cup \ \times$$
multī Lȳdia nōminis
$$— \ —|— \quad \cup \ \cup—\| —\cup\cup \ |—\cup\times$$
    Rōmānā viguī clārior Īliā."

$$— \ — \ | \quad — \quad \cup \quad \cup|— \ \cup \ \times$$
"Mē nunc Thressa Chloē regit,
$$— \ — \ | \ — \ \cup \quad \cup \ — \| — \ \cup \ \cup| — \quad \cup \ \times$$
10   dulcēs docta modōs et citharae sciēns,
$$— \quad —| \ — \quad \cup \ \cup|— \quad \cup \ \times$$
prō quā nōn metuam morī,
$$— \quad —| — \quad \cup \ \cup \ — \|— \ \cup \quad \cup \ |— \ \cup \ \times$$
    sī parcent animae fāta superstitī."

$$— \quad — \ |— \ \cup \ \cup| \ — \ \cup \ \times$$
"Mē torret face mūtuā
$$— \ —|— \ \cup \quad \cup— \|—\cup\cup \ | \ — \ \cup \ \times$$
    Thūrīnī Calais fīlius Ornytī,
$$— \quad —| — \quad \cup\cup|— \quad \cup \ \times$$
15 prō quō bis patiar morī,
$$— \quad — \ |— \quad \cup\cup \ —\|— \ \cup \quad \cup \ |— \ \cup\times$$
    sī parcent puerō fāta superstitī."

---

¹ The letter -y, taken from the Greek alphabet, was often considered a "long" vowel, as here and in lines 7 and 20. But it is "short" in line 14's *Ornytī* and in *Cyprum* in *Odes* III.26, line 9.

```
       —  —|—  ᴗ  ᴗ|—  ᴗ  x
    "Quid sī prisca redit Venus
         —  —|—  ᴗ  ᴗ — ‖— ᴗ  ᴗ|—ᴗx
        dīductōsque iugō cōgit aēneō?
     —  — | — ᴗ  ᴗ|—  ᴗx
    Sī flāv(a) excutitur Chloē
         ——|—  ᴗ  ᴗ —‖ — ᴗᴗ|—  ᴗ x
20      reiectaeque patet iānua Lȳdiae?"

       —   — | — ᴗ  ᴗ| —  ᴗ x
    "Quamquam sīdere pulchrior
         — — | — ᴗ  ᴗ—‖— ᴗ   ᴗ | — ᴗ  x
        ille (e)st, tū levior cortic(e) et improbō
     ——|— ᴗᴗ | — ᴗx
    īrācundior Hadriā,
         — — |— ᴗ  ᴗ  — ‖ —  ᴗ  ᴗ|— ᴗ x
        tēcum vīver(e) amem, tēc(um) obeam libēns!"
```

TRANSLATION

"As long as I was pleasing to you
  nor was some preferred youth putting his arms
on your fair neck,
  I flourished more blessed than a king of the Persians."

5 "As long as you did not burn more because of another
    nor was Lydia behind Chloe,
Lydia of much renown,
    I flourished more famous than Roman Ilia."

"Thracian Chloe now rules me,
10   learned in sweet measures and knowledgeable of the lyre,
for whom I will not fear to die,
    if the fates spare her life and let her survive."

"Calais, the son of Ornytus from Thurii,
    burns me with a shared torch,
15 for whom I will endure dying twice,
    if the fates spare the boy and let him survive."

"What if old Love returns
    and forces the separated ones under a bronze yoke?
If fiery Chloe is shaken out
20   and the door of/to rejected Lydia stands open?"

"Although he is more handsome than a star,
    you more fickle than a cork and
more hot-tempered than the rough Adriatic Sea,
    with you I would love to live, with you I would willingly die."

POINTS TO PONDER
Hor. *Odes* III. 9

1. The suggestion that she formerly preferred him may be meant to "needle" her about his present absence from her bed. It may also reflect male bravado, accurate or misguided.

2. Possible responses include that Lydia's "needle" may be found in her suggestion that he was to blame for the break up and in her description of herself as *multī . . . nominis*. These words imply that Chloe, his current flame, is by contrast an unknown. Lydia's *arsistī* is a stronger expression than his *grātus eram* too. Her reference to "Roman Ilia" outdoes his to a "King of the Persians" because Rhea Silvia (= Ilia) made love with the god Mars and then bore Romulus and Remus, the founders of Rome. Hence she was among the most famous of all Roman women.

3. The assertion that her new love is <u>mutual</u> may imply that his was one-sided (or even merely purchased?). The assertion that her lover is from a respectable Roman family may imply that his is only an unknown and/or readily available woman of the streets. The assertion that she would die twice (*bis*) makes her statement stronger than his.

4. The phrase *iugum aēneum* (bronze yoke) probably symbolizes both the yoke of love (Venus' power is irresistible) and the yoke of subjugation under which Romans forced conquered warriors to walk (the lovers thus admit their defeat at the hands of the powerful goddess).

5. Some readers think the winner is the man, for he speaks first, establishes the details of the conversation and she agrees to the reconciliation in the poem's final line. Others view the winner as Lydia, for she consistently wins the "capping" contest, and has the last word. No one wins, say still others, for the obvious competition between the two and the storms of their relationship are the seeds of its own destruction.

HORACE *Odes* III. 26 Unmodified

Vīxī puellīs nūper idōneus
et mīlitāvī nōn sine glōriā;
    nunc arma dēfunctumque bellō
        barbiton hic pariēs habēbit,

5   laevum marīnae quī Veneris latus
custōdit. Hīc, hīc pōnite lūcida
    fūnālia et vectēs et arcūs
        oppositīs foribus mināces.

Ō quae beātam dīva tenēs Cyprum et
10 Memphin carentem Sīthoniā nive,
    rēgīna, sublīmī flagellō
        tange Chloēn semel arrogantem.

HORACE *Odes* III. 26 Unmodified. Meter: Alcaic Stanza

```
—|—  ⌣|— —‖ — ⌣  ⌣|— ⌣ ×
```
Vīxī puellīs nūper idōneus
```
—| — ⌣|— —‖ —   ⌣ ⌣ | — ⌣×
```
et mīlitāvī nōn sine glōriā;
```
    — |—  ⌣| — — | —   ⌣ | — ×
```
   nunc arma dēfunctumque bellō
```
    — ⌣  ⌣ | —  ⌣ ⌣|— ⌣| — ×
```
   barbiton hic pariēs habēbit,

```
—|—    ⌣|— —‖ — ⌣  ⌣|— ⌣ ×
```
5 laevum marīnae quī Veneris latus
```
—|— ⌣ | —   — ‖ — ⌣⌣| — ⌣ ×
```
custōdit. Hīc, hīc pōnite lūcida
```
    —|—⌣| —   —|— ⌣ |— ×
```
   fūnāli(a) et vectēs et arcūs
```
    —  ⌣ ⌣|—  ⌣ ⌣|—  ⌣ |—×
```
   oppositīs foribus mināces.

```
—| —    ⌣|— — ‖ —⌣  ⌣|—   ⌣   ×
```
Ō quae beātam dīva tenēs Cypr(um) et
```
 — | —  ⌣| — — ‖— ⌣ ⌣|— ⌣ ×
```
10 Memphin carentem Sīthoniā nive,
```
    —|—⌣| —   —|—  ⌣ |— ×
```
   rēgīna, sublīmī flagellō
```
    — ⌣    ⌣|—  ⌣  ⌣|— ⌣| —  ×
```
   tange Chloēn semel arrogantem.

TRANSLATION

      I lived recently fit for the girls
      and I soldiered not without glory;
           now this wall will hold my weapons and my lyre
                retired from war

5   (this wall) which guards the left flank of sea-born Venus.
      Here, here put the burning
           torches and crowbars and bows
                threatening to blocking doors.

      O you who hold as a goddess blessed Cyprus and
10   Memphis lacking Sithonian snow,
           O queen, touch with your uplifted whip
                Chloe scornful just this once.

POINTS TO PONDER
Hor. *Odes* III. 26

1. The poet has been a "soldier" in the army of Venus. She is his queen (*rēgīna*), and he dedicates his gear to her and prays to her.

2. If this poem is interpreted as a dedicatory prayer (cf. the poem's introductory remarks) seeking greater success in his field of endeavor (love), then the fact that the torches are still aflame may imply his readiness to continue as Love's warrior.

3. An obvious similarity between the situation of the two poems lies in the break up of an affair and the end of a relationship. A clear difference is in the poet's engagement in the situation, for Horace seems much more detached about the disintegration. He is dispassionate while Catullus is all passion, he asks Venus only to touch (*tangere*) Chloe as discipline while Catullus chronicles a series of repeated sufferings for Lesbia. The Horatian poem displays all the careful control that Catullus admonishes himself to (re)gain. Consequently, readers often find Catullus' poem to be more immediate, emotional, impulsive and transparent while Horace's is more **IRONIC** and detached. Catullus' poem reflects youthful inexperience and initial hurt; Horace's, maturity and experience in relationships.

OVID *Amōrēs* I. 5 Unmodified (*Expurgated*)

Aestus erat, mediamque diēs exēgerat hōram;
    adposuī mediō membra levanda torō.
Pars adaperta fuit, pars altera clausa fenestrae;
    quāle ferē silvae lūmen habēre solent,
5 quālia sublūcent fugiente crepuscula Phoebō,
    aut ubi nox abiit, nec tamen orta diēs.
Illa verēcundīs lux est praebenda puellīs,
    quā timidus latebrās spēret habēre pudor.
Ecce, Corinna venit, tunicā vēlāta recinctā,
10   candida dīviduā colla tegente comā —
quāliter in thalamōs fāmōsa Semīramis īsse
    dīcitur, et multīs Lāis amāta virīs.
Dēripuī tunicam — nec multum rāra nocēbat;
    pugnābat tunicā sed tamen illa tegī.
15 Quae cum ita pugnāret, tamquam quae vincere nollet,
    victa est nōn aegrē prōditiōne suā.
Ut stetit ante oculōs positō vēlāmine nostrōs,
    in tōtō nusquam corpore menda fuit.
    . . . .
20   . . . .
    . . . .
    . . . .
Singula quid referam? Nil nōn laudābile vīdī
    et nūdam pressī corpus ad usque meum.
25 Cētera quis nescit? Lassī requiēvimus ambō.
    Prōveniant mediī sīc mihi saepe diēs!

OVID *Amōrēs* I. 5 Unmodified (*Expurgated*)
Meter: Elegiac Couplet

$$— \cup \cup | — \cup \cup | — \cup \cup | — | — \cup \cup | — \times$$
Aestus erat, mediamque diēs exēgerat hōram;
$$— \cup \cup | — \cup \cup | — \| — \cup \cup | — \cup \cup | \times$$
adposuī mediō membra levanda torō.
$$— \cup \cup | — \cup \cup | — | — \cup \cup | — \cup \cup | — \times$$
Pars adaperta fuit, pars altera clausa fenestrae;
$$— \cup \cup | — | — \| — \cup \cup | — \cup \cup | \times$$
quāle ferē silvae lūmen habēre solent,
$$— \cup \cup | — — | — \cup \cup | — \cup \cup | — \cup \cup | — \times$$
5   quālia sublūcent fugiente crepuscula Phoebō,
$$— \cup \cup | — \cup \cup | — \| — \cup \cup | — \cup \cup | \times$$
aut ubi nox abiit, nec tamen orta diēs.
$$— \cup \cup | — — | — — | — — \cup \cup | — \times$$
Illa verēcundīs lux est praebenda puellīs,
$$— \cup \cup | — \cup \cup | — \| — \cup \cup | — \cup \cup | \times$$
quā timidus latebrās spēret habēre pudor.
$$— \cup \cup | — \cup \cup | — \cup \cup | — | — \cup \cup | — \times$$
Ecce, Corinna venit, tunicā vēlāta recinctā,
$$— \cup \cup | — \cup \cup | — \| — \cup \cup | — \cup \cup | \times$$
10 candida dīviduā colla tegente comā —
$$— \cup \cup | — \cup \cup | — | — \cup \cup | — \cup \cup | — \times$$
quāliter in thalamōs fāmōsa Semīramis īsse
$$— \cup \cup | — — | — \| — \cup \cup | — \cup \cup | \times$$
dīcitur, et multīs Lāis amāta virīs.
$$— \cup \cup | — \cup \cup | — | — — | — \cup \cup | — \times$$
Dēripuī tunicam — nec multum rāra nocēbat;
$$— — | — \cup \cup | — \| — \cup \cup | — \cup \cup | \times$$
pugnābat tunicā sed tamen illa tegī.
$$— \cup \cup | — — | — — | — — \cup \cup | — \times$$
15 Quae c(um) ita pugnāret, tamquam quae vincere nollet,
$$— — | — — | — \| — \cup \cup | — \cup \cup | \times$$
victa (e)st nōn aegrē prōditiōne suā.
$$— \cup \cup | — \cup \cup | — \cup \cup | — | — \cup \cup | — \times$$
Ut stetit ant(e) oculōs positō vēlāmine nostrōs,
$$— — | — | — \| — \cup \cup | — \cup \cup | \times$$
in tōtō nusquam corpore menda fuit.

20 ....
....
....

```
   —  ⏑ ⏑|  —     ⏑ ⏑| —    — |—   — |— ⏑ ⏑ | — ×
```
Singula quid referam? Nīl nōn laudābile vīdī
```
   —    — |—    — |—‖ —   ⏑  ⏑ |—   ⏑   ⏑|×
```
et nūdam pressī corpus ad usque meum.

25
```
   —  ⏑⏑|  —    — |—    — |—  ⏑  ⏑|—⏑  ⏑ |—  ×
```
Cētera quis nescit? Lassī requiēvimus ambō.
```
   —   ⏑ ⏑|—    ⏑ ⏑|—‖ —   ⏑ ⏑| —   ⏑  ⏑|×
```
Prōveniant mediī sīc mihi saepe diēs!

UNIT REVIEW ANSWER KEY

TRANSLATION (*Expurgated*)

It was hot, and the day had passed the middle hour;
    I placed my limbs to be relieved in the middle of the bed.
Part of the window was opened, the other part (was) closed;
    the sort of light woods generally are accustomed to have,
5   the sort of twilight that shines faintly when Phoebus is fleeing
    or when night has gone nor yet has day risen.
That light must be provided to bashful girls
    in which timid modesty may hope to have hiding places.
Look, Corinna comes, dressed in a loosened tunic,
10   with her parted hair covering her fair neck,
just like notorious Semiramis was said to go into bedrooms,
    and Lais loved by many men.
I tore off the tunic; nor was the scanty thing doing much harm
    but she still was struggling to be covered by the tunic;
15   and since she was struggling like a woman who would not wish to overcome,
    she was overcome not with difficulty by her own betrayal/treason.
As she stood there before our eyes with the garment laid aside,
    nowhere on her whole body was there a flaw.
    ....
20   ....
    ....
    ....
Why should I repeat her individual features? I saw nothing not praiseworthy,
    and I pressed the nude girl tightly to my own body.
25   Who does not know the rest? Worn out, we began to rest up – both of us.
    May mid-days like this often happen for me!

POINTS TO PONDER
Ovid *Amōrēs* I. 5

1. Many readers find the poem playful and sensuous but not tender. The relationship is not so much the focus of the poem as is the meeting itself and the description of what transpired.

2. Corinna's perspective is represented by the poet only in lines 15–16 when he describes her resistance as pretended and when line 25 includes both him and her in the plural forms *Lassī requiēvimus ambō*.

3. Some readers think that the visit was prearranged because of the way Corinna was dressed when she arrived (lines 9–10), because of her moderate resistance (lines 15–16) and because she came to his residence. Others point out that the details of the first two of these causes are reported from his point of view and may not reflect her viewpoint.

4. IRONY is found in the phrases *verēcundīs . . . puellīs* and *timidus pudor* since a girl who arrives at a man's residence *tunica vēlāta recincta* (dressed in an untied tunic) with her hair down (line 10) would be considered neither shy (*verēcunda*) nor timidly chaste (having *timidus pudor*).

In this poem, Ovid reflects upon a pleasant afternoon spent in the company of his lover, Corinna. Ovid's detailed description of the quality of the light serves as an anticipatory prelude to his reminiscence. Similarly, his intimate recollection of Corinna's physical characteristics (step-by-step, as it were), climaxing in trio of exclamations (lines 21–22), reinforces the languid mood of the poem.

OVID *Amōrēs* I. 5 Unmodified (*Unexpurgated*)

    Aestus erat, mediamque diēs exēgerat hōram;
        adposuī mediō membra levanda torō.
    Pars adaperta fuit, pars altera clausa fenestrae;
        quāle ferē silvae lūmen habēre solent,
5   quālia sublūcent fugiente crepuscula Phoebō,
        aut ubi nox abiit, nec tamen orta diēs.
    Illa verēcundīs lux est praebenda puellīs,
        quā timidus latebrās spēret habēre pudor.
    Ecce, Corinna venit, tunicā vēlāta recinctā,
10   candida dīviduā colla tegente comā —
    quāliter in thalamōs fāmōsa Semīramis īsse
        dīcitur, et multīs Lāis amāta virīs.
    Dēripuī tunicam — nec multum rāra nocēbat;
        pugnābat tunicā sed tamen illa tegī.
15   Quae cum ita pugnāret, tamquam quae vincere nollet,
        victa est nōn aegrē prōditiōne suā.
    Ut stetit ante oculōs positō vēlāmine nostrōs,
        in tōtō nusquam corpore menda fuit.
    Quōs umerōs, quālēs vīdī tetigīque lacertōs!
20   Forma papillārum quam fuit apta premī!
    Quam castīgātō plānus sub pectore venter!
        Quantum et quāle latus! Quam iuvenāle femur!
    Singula quid referam? Nil nōn laudābile vīdī
        et nūdam pressī corpus ad usque meum.
25   Cētera quis nescit? Lassī requiēvimus ambō.
    Prōveniant mediī sīc mihi saepe diēs!

OVID *Amōrēs* I. 5 Unmodified (*Unexpurgated*)
Meter: Elegiac Couplet

```
— ∪ ∪|— ∪ ∪|— ∪ ∪|— —|—∪ ∪ | — x
```
Aestus erat, mediamque diēs exēgerat hōram;
```
— ∪ ∪|— ∪ ∪|—‖ — ∪ ∪|— ∪ ∪| x
```
adposuī mediō membra levanda torō.
```
— ∪ ∪|— ∪ ∪|— | —∪ ∪| — ∪ ∪|— x
```
Pars adaperta fuit, pars altera clausa fenestrae;
```
— ∪ ∪|— —| —‖ — ∪ ∪|— ∪ ∪| x
```
quāle ferē silvae lūmen habēre solent,
```
— ∪∪| — —|— ∪ ∪|— ∪ ∪| — ∪ ∪| — x
```
5 quālia sublūcent fugiente crepuscula Phoebō,
```
— ∪ ∪| — ∪ ∪|—‖ — ∪ ∪| —∪ ∪|x
```
aut ubi nox abiit, nec tamen orta diēs.
```
—∪ ∪|——| — —| — —| — ∪ ∪|— x
```
Illa verēcundīs lux est praebenda puellīs,
```
— ∪ ∪ |— ∪ ∪|—‖ — ∪ ∪|— ∪ ∪| x
```
quā timidus latebrās spēret habēre pudor.
```
— ∪ ∪|— ∪ ∪|— ∪ ∪|— —|—∪ ∪|— x
```
Ecce, Corinna venit, tunicā vēlāta recinctā,
```
— ∪ ∪| — ∪ ∪|—‖— ∪ ∪| — ∪ ∪|x
```
10 candida dīviduā colla tegente comā —
```
— ∪ ∪ |— ∪ ∪| —|— ∪ ∪| —∪ ∪| — x
```
quāliter in thalamōs fāmōsa Semīramis īsse
```
—∪ ∪ | — — |—‖ —∪ ∪|— ∪ ∪|x
```
dīcitur, et multīs Lāis amāta virīs.
```
— ∪ ∪|— ∪ ∪| — | — —|— ∪ ∪|— x
```
Dēripuī tunicam — nec multum rāra nocēbat;
```
— —|— ∪ ∪|—‖ — ∪ ∪|— ∪ ∪| x
```
pugnābat tunicā sed tamen illa tegī.
```
— ∪ ∪ |— —|— —|— — — ∪ ∪| — x
```
15 Quae c(um) ita pugnāret, tamquam quae vincere nollet,
```
— — | — —| —‖ — ∪ ∪|—∪ ∪|x
```
victa (e)st nōn aegrē prōditiōne suā.
```
— ∪ ∪ |— ∪ ∪|— ∪ ∪|— —| — ∪ ∪| — x
```
Ut stetit ant(e) oculōs positō vēlāmine nostrōs,
```
— —|— —| — ‖ —∪ ∪|— ∪ ∪|x
```
in tōtō nusquam corpore menda fuit.

Quōs umerōs, quālēs vīdī tetigīque lacertōs!
20 Forma papillārum quam fuit apta premī!
Quam castīgātō plānus sub pectore venter!
Quant(um) et quāle latus! Quam iuvenāle femur!
Singula quid referam? Nīl nōn laudābile vīdī
et nūdam pressī corpus ad usque meum.
25 Cētera quis nescit? Lassī requiēvimus ambō.
Prōveniant mediī sīc mihi saepe diēs!

TRANSLATION (*Unexpurgated*)

    It was hot, and the day had passed the middle hour;
        I placed my limbs to be relieved in the middle of the bed.
    Part of the window was opened, the other part (was) closed;
        the sort of light woods generally are accustomed to have,
5   the sort of twilight that shines faintly when Phoebus is fleeing
        or when night has gone nor yet has day risen.
    That light must be provided to bashful girls
        in which timid modesty may hope to have hiding places.
    Look, Corinna comes, dressed in a loosened tunic,
10   with her parted hair covering her fair neck,
    just like notorious Semiramis was said to go into bedrooms,
        and Lais loved by many men.
    I tore off the tunic; nor was the scanty thing doing much harm
        but she still was struggling to be covered by the tunic;
15   and since she was struggling like a woman who would not wish to overcome,
        she was overcome not with difficulty by her own betrayal/treason.
    As she stood there before our eyes with the garment laid aside,
        nowhere on her whole body was there a flaw.
    What shoulders, what sort of upper arms did I see and touch!
20   The shape of her breasts – how fit to be pressed it was!
    How flat her tummy beneath her well-muscled chest!
        The size and quality of her flank! How youthful her thigh!
    Why should I repeat her individual features? I saw nothing not praiseworthy,
        and I pressed the nude girl tightly to my own body.
25   Who does not know the rest? Worn out, we began to rest up – both of us.
        May mid-days like this often happen for me!

POINTS TO PONDER
Ovid *Amōrēs* I. 5

1. Many readers find the poem playful and sensuous but not tender. The relationship is not so much the focus of the poem as is the meeting itself and the description of what transpired.

2. Corinna's perspective is represented by the poet only in lines 15–16 when he describes her resistance as pretended and when line 25 includes both him and her in the plural forms *Lassī requiēvimus ambō*.

3. Some readers think that the visit was prearranged because of the way Corinna was dressed when she arrived (lines 9–10), because of her moderate resistance (lines 15–16) and because she came to his residence. Others point out that the details of the first two of these causes are reported from <u>his</u> point of view and may not reflect <u>her</u> viewpoint.

4. **Irony** is found in the phrases *verēcundīs . . . puellīs* and *timidus pudor* since a girl who arrives at a man's residence *tunica vēlāta recincta* (dressed in an untied tunic) with her hair down (line 10) would be considered neither shy (*verēcunda*) nor timidly chaste (having *timidus pudor*).

5. Most readers find the lack of specific detail in line 25 about the act of love evidence of the poet's tasteful description, and hence judge the description to be accurate.

UNIT REVIEW ANSWER KEY

STUDENT MATERIALS FOR OVID AMŌRĒS I. 5 UNMODIFIED (UNEXPURGATED)

TEXTUAL MATTERS

1. Note the now familiar first word–last word arrangement in line 1.
2. In line 3 there is an ELLIPSIS of *fenestrae* with the initial *pars,* and of *fuit* with *clausa.*
3. In lines 5–8, the adjectives *quālia, verēcundīs* and *timidus* are separated from their nouns.
4. In lines 9–10 be sure to pay attention to the difference in the -a endings.
5. In line 14 note the delayed position of the phrase *sed tamen illa.*
6. *Nostrōs* is separated from *oculōs* in line 17.
7. Note the SYNCHESIS in line 21.
8. In line 24 *ad usque* = *usque ad.*
9. Line 26 illustrates both the separation of *mediī* from its noun *diēs* and the familiar first word–last word arrangement.

POINTS TO PONDER

1. What adjective most fittingly describes this poem—playful? tender? sensuous?
2. The events of the poem are told from his point of view. Is Corinna's perspective represented at all?
3. Was the visit pre-arranged or unexpected? Is it significant that she came to his residence?
4. Explain the IRONY in the phrases *verēcundīs . . . puellīs* and *timidus . . . pudor* in lines 7–8.
5. In discussing this poem, the commentators M. Balme and J. Morwood describe it as the first in Latin literature that "simply describes love-making" and add, "It is in no way a prurient piece. The mood is one of relaxed hedonism." Are their characterization and assertions about prurience and mood accurate? What in the poem supports this view?

OVID *Amōrēs* I. 9 Unmodified

Mīlitat omnis amāns, et habet sua castra Cupīdō;
   Attice, crēde mihi, mīlitat omnis amāns.
Quae bellō est habilis, Venerī quoque convenit aetās.
   Turpe senex mīles, turpe senīlis amor.
5   Quōs petiēre ducēs animōs in mīlite fortī,
   hōs petit in sociō bella puella virō:
pervigilant ambō; terrā requiescit uterque—
   ille forēs dominae servat, at ille ducis.
Mīlitis officium longa est via; mitte puellam,
10   strenuus exemptō fīne sequētur amāns.
Ībit in adversōs montēs duplicātaque nimbō
   flūmina, congestās exteret ille nivēs,
nec freta pressūrus tumidōs causābitur Eurōs
   aptaque verrendīs sīdera quaeret aquīs.
15   Quis nisi vel mīles vel amāns et frīgora noctis
   et densō mixtās perferet imbre nivēs?
Mittitur infestōs alter speculātor in hostēs;
   in rīvāle oculōs alter, ut hoste, tenet.
Ille gravēs urbēs, hic dūrae līmen amīcae
20   obsidet; hic portās frangit, at ille forēs.
Saepe sopōrātōs invādere profuit hostēs
   caedere et armātā vulgus inerme manū.
Sīc fera Thrēiciī cecidērunt agmina Rhēsī,
   et dominum captī dēseruistis equī.
25   Nempe marītōrum somnīs ūtuntur amantēs,
   et sua sōpītīs hostibus arma movent.
Custōdum transīre manūs vigilumque catervās
   mīlitis et miserī semper amantis opus.
Mars dubius nec certa Venus; victīque resurgunt,
30   quōsque negēs umquam posse iacēre, cadunt.

Ergō dēsidiam quīcumque vocābat amōrem,
　　dēsinat. Ingeniī est experientis Amor.
Ardet in abductā Brīsēide magnus Achillēs —
　　dum licet, Argīvās frangite, Trōes, opēs!
35　Hector ab Andromachēs complexibus ībat ad arma,
　　et, galeam capitī quae daret, uxor erat.
Summa ducum, Atrīdēs, vīsā Priamēide fertur
　　Maenadis effūsīs obstipuisse comīs.
Mars quoque dēprēnsus fabrīlia vincula sēnsit;
40　　nōtior in caelō fābula nulla fuit.
Ipse ego segnis eram discinctaque in ōtia nātus;
　　mollierant animōs lectus et umbra meōs.
Impulit ignāvum formōsae cūra puellae
　　iussit et in castrīs aera merēre suīs.
45　Inde vidēs agilem nocturnaque bella gerentem.
　　Quī nōlet fierī dēsidiōsus, amet!

OVID *Amōrēs* I. 9 Unmodified

Mīlitat omnis amāns, et habet sua castra Cupīdō;
　　Attice, crēde mihi[1], mīlitat omnis amāns.
Quae bellō (e)st habilis, Venerī quoque convenit aetās.
　　Turpe senex mīles, turpe senīlis amor.
5　Quōs petiēre ducēs animōs in mīlite fortī,
　　hōs petit in sociō bella puella virō:
pervigilant ambō; terrā requiescit uterque —
　　ille forēs dominae servat, at ille ducis.
Mīlitis officium longa (e)st via; mitte puellam,
10　　strenuus exemptō fīne sequētur amāns.
Ībit in adversōs montēs duplicātaque nimbō
　　flūmina, congestās exteret ille nivēs,
nec freta pressūrus tumidōs causābitur Eurōs
　　aptaque verrendīs sīdera quaeret aquīs.
15　Quis nisi vel mīles vel amāns et frīgora noctis
　　et densō mixtās perferet imbre nivēs?
Mittitur infestōs alter speculātor in hostēs;
　　in rīvāl(e) oculōs alter, ut hoste, tenet.

---

[1] Again, the final -ī in *mihī* is long. Cf. Catullus 8. lines 11 and 15.

UNIT REVIEW ANSWER KEY

```
  — ᴗ   ᴗ|  — —|  —   — |  — —|—  ᴗ   ᴗ|— ×
```
Ille gravēs urbēs, hic dūrae līmen amīcae
```
     — ᴗ  ᴗ |  —  —|—‖  —  ᴗ  ᴗ|—  ᴗ  ᴗ |x
```
20   obsidet; hic portās frangit, at ille forēs.
```
    —  ᴗ  ᴗ|—  —|—  —|—  ᴗ  ᴗ|—  ᴗ  ᴗ| — ×
```
Saepe sopōrātōs invādere profuit hostēs
```
     —  ᴗ   ᴗ |  ——|—‖ —  ᴗ  ᴗ |— ᴗ   ᴗ| ×
```
caeder(e) et armātā vulgus inerme manū.
```
  —  ᴗ  ᴗ|  —  — ᴗᴗ|—  ᴗ  ᴗ|—  — |—  ᴗ  ᴗ|  — ×
```
Sīc fera Thrēiciī cecidērunt agmina Rhēsī,
```
    —  —  ᴗ|—  — |—‖ — ᴗ  ᴗ|— ᴗ   ᴗ|x
```
et dominum captī dēseruistis equī.
```
   —    ᴗ   ᴗ|—  —|—   — |  — —|— ᴗ   ᴗ|  — ×
```
25   Nempe marītōrum somnīs ūtuntur amantēs,
```
    —  ᴗᴗ|——|—‖ — ᴗ  ᴗ|—   ᴗ    ᴗ| ×
```
et sua sōpītīs hostibus arma movent.
```
   —  —|—   —|— ᴗ   ᴗ|—  ᴗ  ᴗ|—  ᴗ    ᴗ|— ×
```
Custōdum transīre manūs vigilumque catervās
```
  — ᴗᴗ  |—  ᴗ  ᴗ |—‖—  ᴗ  ᴗ | —  ᴗ   ᴗ ×
```
mīlitis et miserī semper amantis opus.
```
  —   ᴗ  ᴗ |—  —|— ᴗ  ᴗ|—  —|—  ᴗ  ᴗ|—  ×
```
Mars dubius nec certa Venus; victīque resurgunt,
```
   —   ᴗ    ᴗ|—  — |— ‖  — ᴗ  ᴗ|— ᴗ    ᴗ|x
```
30   quōsque negēs umquam posse iacēre, cadunt.
```
   —  —|— ᴗ  ᴗ|—  —|— ᴗ  ᴗ|—  ᴗ   ᴗ |—×
```
Ergō dēsidiam quīcumque vocābat amōrem,
```
   — ᴗ  ᴗ |— ᴗ  ᴗ|—   ‖ — ᴗᴗ|— ᴗ  ᴗ| ×
```
<u>dēsinat. Ingeniī (e)st experientis Amor.</u>
```
   —  ᴗ   ᴗ|— —|—  —|—ᴗ  ᴗ|—   ᴗ  ᴗ| — ×
```
Ardet in abductā Brīsēide magnus Achillēs —
```
    — ᴗ  ᴗ|— —| ‖ — ᴗ  ᴗ| — ᴗ  ᴗ| ×
```
dum licet, Argīvās frangite, Trōes, opēs!
```
  — ᴗ  ᴗ | — ᴗ   ᴗ |   —|—  ᴗ  ᴗ|— ᴗᴗ| — ×
```
35   Hector ab Andromachēs complexibus ībat ad arma,
```
   — ᴗ  ᴗ|—  ᴗ  ᴗ|—‖ — ᴗ  ᴗ|— ᴗ  ᴗ| x
```
et, galeam capitī quae daret, uxor erat.
```
  —   ᴗ   ᴗ|  —  —|—   —| ᴗᴗ |—ᴗᴗ|  — ×
```
Summa duc(um), Atrīdēs, vīsā Priamēide fertur
```
   — ᴗ  ᴗ |——|—‖ — ᴗ  ᴗ|— ᴗ  ᴗ| ×
```
Maenadis effūsīs obstipuisse comīs.

$$\text{—} \cup \cup | \text{—} \text{—} | \text{—} \quad \text{—} | \text{—} \cup \cup | \text{—} \cup \cup | \text{—} \times$$
Mars quoque dēprēnsus fabrīlia vincula sēnsit;
$$\text{—} \cup \cup | \text{—} \quad \text{—} | \text{—} \| \text{—} \cup \cup | \text{—} \cup \cup | \times$$
40 nōtior in caelō fābula nulla fuit.
$$\text{—} \quad \cup \cup | \text{—} \cup \cup | \text{—} \quad \text{—} | \text{—} \cup \cup | \text{—} \cup \cup | \text{—} \times$$
Ips(e) ego segnis eram discinctaqu(e) in ōtia nātus;
$$\text{—} \quad \cup \cup | \text{—} \cup \cup | \text{—} \| \text{—} \cup \cup | \text{—} \cup \cup | \times$$
mollierant animōs lectus et umbra meōs.
$$\text{—} \quad \cup \cup | \text{—} \text{—} | \text{—} | \text{—} \text{—} | \text{—} \cup \cup | \text{—} \times$$
Impulit ignāvum formōsae cūra puellae
$$\text{—} \quad \cup \cup | \text{—} \text{—} | \text{—} \| \text{—} \cup \cup | \text{—} \cup \cup | \times$$
iussit et in castrīs aera merēre suīs.
$$\text{—} \quad \cup \cup | \text{—} \cup \cup | \text{—} \text{—} | \text{—} \cup \cup | \text{—} \cup \cup | \text{—} \times$$
45 Inde vidēs agilem nocturnaque bella gerentem.
$$\text{—} \quad \text{—} | \text{—} \quad \cup \cup | \text{—} \| \text{—} \cup \cup | \text{—} \cup \quad \cup | \times$$
Quī nōlet fierī dēsidiōsus, amet!

TRANSLATION

    Every lover is a soldier, and Cupid has his own camp;
        Atticus, believe me, every lover is a soldier.
    The time of life, which is suitable for war, suits Venus also.
        A disgraceful thing is an old soldier, a disgraceful thing is an old man's love.
5   The courage which a general sought in a brave soldier,
        this a pretty girl seeks in her male companion:
    both are on guard all night, each begins to rest on the ground;
        that one guards his mistress' door, but that one his general's.
    The soldier's task is a long road: dispatch a girl,
10   the vigorous lover will follow with border removed;
    he'll go into obstructing mountains and streams doubled by a cloudburst,
        that man will trample over piled up snow,
    and, about to be on straits, he will not plead as excuse the swell-causing winds of Eurus
        or ask for weather suitable for skimming over the waters.
15   Who except either a soldier or lover will endure both the chills of the night
        and snow mixed with heavy hail?
    One is sent as a spy on deadly enemies,
        the other keeps his eyes on a rival, as on a foe.
    That one lays siege to important cities, this one to the threshold of a hard girlfriend;
20   the one breaks gates, but the other, doors.
    Often it has been useful to attack the enemy buried in sleep
        and to slay an unarmed throng with an armed band.
    In this way the fierce columns of Thracian Rhesus fell,
        and you, O captured horses, deserted your master.
25   Without a doubt lovers employ the dreams of husbands
        and move their weapons when the enemy has been put to sleep.
    It is necessary for the soldier and the wretched lover
        to go past bands of guards and squads of sentinels.
    Mars is uncertain, nor is Venus sure: the overcome rise again
30   and those whom you would deny ever to be able to go down, fall.
    Therefore, whoever was calling love laziness should cease:
        <u>Love is a something of an active character.</u>
    Great Achilles was on fire for Briseis who had been taken away (by Agamemnon) –
        break the Greek defenses while it's allowed, Trojans!
35   Hector used to go to arms from Andromache's embraces
        and his wife was the one to give him his helmet for his head.
    Atreus' son (Agamemnon), the greatest of generals, is said to have been astounded
        when Priam's daughter (Cassandra) was seen with the disheveled hair of a Bacchante.
    Mars also was caught and felt the chains forged (by Vulcan);

40   no tale was more familiar in heaven.
   I myself was slack and born for undisciplined leisure;
      my shady couch had softened my spirit;
   Love for a shapely girl drove me from my laziness
      and ordered me to earn my wages in its camp.
45 From this you see me active and waging the wars of the night.
      Whoever won't want to become lazy – let him be a lover.

POINTS TO PONDER
Ovid *Amōrēs* I. 9

1. Cupid is the lover/warrior's commander as Venus was in *Ode* III. 26. The difference is significant only in gender and gear—Cupid as a male attacks his victims with weapons (arrows) while Venus is Cupid's "Commanding Officer" and generally attacks with strategy and seduction.

2. When a lover plans his campaign, he strives primarily to "overcome" the girl, though he may also need to dislodge a rival for her affection. He rarely is thinking about gaining control over his own desires.

3. The similarity is the basic **METAPHOR** of a lover as a soldier. Some differences are that Horace poses as a retired veteran while Ovid poses as an active campaigner, that Horace briefly mentions his military gear (three implements) while Ovid has an extended description not of gear but of a lover's soldierly activities, and that Horace pleads for Venus to bring Chloe back while Ovid pleads that a lover must be fully as active as a warrior. The effectiveness of each portrayal is largely a matter of the individual reader's taste.

SAMPLE "ALTERNATIVE ASSESSMENT PROJECTS"

Introduction to sample alternative assessment projects

In this *Libellus*, we have provided a variety of questions and exercises relating to each poetry selection. These are meant to help students review grammar and syntax by completing textbook-type exercises and increase their proficiency in translating and interpreting Latin poetry. With these questions and exercises as a template, teachers can assess their students in traditional ways using quizzes and tests. Outside of the classroom, however, job performance assessment rarely takes the form of a quiz or a test. More often, it is a written report, a visual chart or graph, and/or an oral presentation of information to a group—created individually or in a group setting.

An important development stemming from the Standards movement in education has been the recognition of alternative assessment as a valid tool for evaluating student performance and a valuable medium for enabling students to learn these necessary research and social skills. Thus, we felt it would be useful to offer a variety of sample projects which teachers may use as supplemental activities or assessments relating to the material found in the *Libellus*. In addition, these projects round out the Standards-based approach of the *Libellus* by directly addressing Goals 2, 3, 4, and 5 in their entirety.

There are five sample projects in this section. Projects 1 and 2 focus on major Roman historical and literary personages, and they are designed to introduce students to the four main components of projects: research, a written report, a visual enhancement to the written text, and an oral presentation. These first projects are <u>individual</u> projects. Project 3, a timeline, introduces the concept of working in a <u>group</u> to create a visual product. Project 4, important sites in the Roman Empire, adds the additional challenge of a group presentation. Project 5 was designed to help students synthesize their knowledge of poetry following an entire course devoted to the study of Catullus, Horace, and Ovid. In this final project, students were asked to illustrate poetry, to create original poems in the style of the poets, and to read poetry for their peers. Teachers are free to make modifications to these projects according to the more limited scope of this transitional *Libellus*. Each sample project contains a project description, self and/or peer evaluation forms, project grading rubrics, and project evaluation forms.

ROMAN HISTORICAL FIGURES PROJECT　　　　　　　　　　NOMEN_____

Description: In this project, your task will be to learn about an important political figure who lived contemporaneously to Catullus, Horace, or Ovid.

Topics:

Quintus Caecilius Metellus Gaius	Julius Caesar Octavianus
Gaius Julius Caesar	Marcus Antonius
Lucius Cornelius Sulla	Marcus Aemilius Lepidus
Marcus Tullius Cicero	Caius Asinius Pollio
Publius Clodius Pulcher	Marcus Vipsanius Agrippa
Marcus Valerius Messalla	Valerius Messala Corvinus
Marcus Junius Brutus	Tiberius Claudius Nero Caesar
Caius Cassius Longinus	Germanicus Julius Caesar
Cnaeus Pompeius Magnus	Valerius Cato
Marcus Licinius Crassus	Caius Cilnius Maecenas

Sources:
- library and Internet research
- lecture notes from class
    - ** Please acknowledge all sources in a bibliography according to the <u>Chicago Manual of Form and Style</u>.**

Tasks:
- research the life of the historical person assigned
- create a written paper (3–5 pages) about that person
- create a visual element appropriate to your topic
- infuse your paper and/or visual with memorable details
- present the details of your research orally in class, in a short (3–5 minute) presentation.

Paper Parameters:
- length: 2–4 pages of typed text about your topic
- font: Times New Roman, size 12
- spacing: double-spaced
- margins: one-inch, left-ruled
- Title page and Bibliography

Visual:
- size = 8.5" x 11"
- must be appropriate for your topic (e.g. a layout of a battlefield, a picture/bust/statue of the historical figure, a map, etc.)
- must include the 4–6 most important informational details about your person, place, battle, etc. (these points may come from the text of your paper)

DUE DATE FOR ALL PROJECTS: In class on_____. Projects handed in late will be reduced one letter grade per day late. **NO EXCEPTIONS!!**

NOTA BENE: This is an independent project, to be completed on your own without collaborating with another student. (There will be opportunities for collaborative work on other projects.)

SAMPLE "ALTERNATIVE ASSESSMENT PROJECTS"

SELF EVALUATION: ROMAN HISTORICAL FIGURES PROJECT

NOMEN_____ **DIES**_____

1. Please provide an honest assessment of the approximate amount of time (total hours) you spent working on the tasks for this project. Please itemize SPECIFIC tasks which you performed and how long you spent working on each task.

    Tasks include (but you may add others):
    Research
    writing an outline/rough draft
    writing the paper
    creating the visual aid
    presenting the material to the class
    Other tasks (please describe):

2. Please rate the quality and depth of your project according to the rubrics by placing an "X" in the box which best applies.

QUALITY OF PAPER, VISUAL AID, AND ORAL PRESENTATION	SUPERB= included exceptional level of detail; demonstrated considerable effort	ACCEPTABLE= included an adequate amount of detail; demonstrated solid effort	FAIR= included moderate amount of detail; demonstrated some effort	POOR= included some to little detail; represented a hurried project with minimal effort
text includes pertinent dates				
text includes important life cycle events (birth, death, marriage, children)				
text includes 5–8 other important facts (career, travel, personality, habits, contributions)				
visual aid relates to person				
visual aid contains 4–6 important facts				
speaking during oral report was clear, with adequate volume, and at an intelligible speed				
oral report provided information in an organized and understandable presentation				
Aesthetic quality of project (neatness, creativity, beauty)				

3. Please give yourself an overall grade: A   A-   B+   B   B-   C+   C   C-   D+   D   F
    Please explain why you gave yourself the grade you did in a **minimum** of 3–5 sentences below:

4. What aspects of the project should be altered so that it may be more understandable or work more smoothly in the future?

ROMAN HISTORICAL FIGURES GRADING RUBRIC   NOMEN_____

OPTIME = demonstrated exceptional understanding / proficiency / effort / level of detail
BENE = demonstrated acceptable understanding / proficiency / effort / level of detail
SATIS = demonstrated moderate understanding / proficiency / effort / level of detail; could / should have done more work
NON SATIS = demonstrated some or little understanding / proficiency / effort / level of detail; could / should have done considerably more work

	OPTIME	BENE	SATIS	NON SATIS
QUALITY OF INFORMATION				
important dates/events included (50 pts.) (life cycle, career, personality)	(50–44)	(43–37)	(36–30)	
additional appropriate (20 pts.) dates/events included	(20–17)	(16–13)	(12–8)	
accuracy of information (30 pts.)	(30–26)	(25–21)	(20–16)	
VISUAL AID				
relates to person (25 pts.)	(25–22)	(21–18)	(17–13)	
contains 4–6 impt. facts (25 pts.)	(25–22)	(21–18)	(17–13)	
ORAL PRESENTATION				
quality of voice (30 pts.) volume, clarity, speed	(30–26)	(25–21)	(20–16)	
organized presentation (20 pts.)	(20–17)	(16–12)	(12–8)	
AESTHETIC FEATURES				
neatness of presentation (5 pts.)	(5–4)	(3–2)	(1)	
creative presentation (5 pts.)	(5–4)	(3–2)	(1)	
spelling, punctuation, grammar (5 pts.)	(5–4)	(3–2)	(1)	
exceptional communication of ideas (5 pts.)	(5–4)	(3–2)	(1)	
exceptional detail of information (5 pts.)	(5–4)	(3–2)	(1)	

TOTAL POINTS (225 possible)
GRADE ADJUSTMENT (ON TIME?_____; # DAYS LATE_____)
COMMENTS:

SAMPLE "ALTERNATIVE ASSESSMENT PROJECTS"

PROJECT EVALUATION: ROMAN HISTORICAL FIGURES

1. Do you feel this project was more or less useful than individual readings, followed by a lecture and a test? Please make one-two comments on the positive/negative aspects of the project vs. lecture.

2. Did you spend more or less time preparing for the project than you would have for readings and a test? How did your use of preparation time differ?

3. Do your feel working with your classmates would have helped or hindered the project?

4. Tell me something new that you learned (about yourself or the material) as a result of this project, that you did not expect.

5. What other kinds of projects do you think would be fun and interesting to explore?

ROMAN LITERARY FIGURES PROJECT   NOMEN_____

Description: In this project, your task will be to learn about an important literary figure who either had an influence upon or lived contemporaneously to Catullus, Horace, or Ovid.

Topics:
Caecilius	Theocritus	Sextus Propertius
Caius Licinius Calvus	Alcaeus	Albius Tibullus
Caius Helvius Cinna	Sappho	Aristius Fuscus
Caius Asinius Gallus	Publius Vergilius Maro	Lucius Varius Rufus
Callimachus	Quintilius Varus	Sulpicia

Sources:
- library and Internet research
- lecture notes from class
    - ** Please acknowledge all sources in a bibliography according to the *Chicago Manual of Form and Style*.**

Tasks:
- research the life of the literary person assigned
- create a written paper (3–5 pages) about that person
- create a visual element appropriate to your topic
- infuse your paper and/or visual with memorable details
- present the details of your research orally in class, in a short (3–5 minute) presentation.

Paper Parameters:
- length: 2–4 pages of typed text about your topic
- font: Times New Roman, size 12
- spacing: double-spaced
- margins: one-inch, left-ruled
- Title page and Bibliography

Visual:
- size = 8.5" x 11"
- must be appropriate for your topic (e.g. a layout of a battlefield, a picture/bust/statue of the figure, a map, etc.)
- must include the 4–6 most important informational details about your person, place, battle, etc. (these points may come from the text of your paper)

DUE DATE FOR ALL PROJECTS: In class on_____. Projects handed in late will be reduced one letter grade per day late. **NO EXCEPTIONS!!**

NOTA BENE: This is an independent project, to be completed on your own without collaborating with another student. (There will be opportunities for collaborative work on other projects.)

Grading: 225 points total
- 100 paper
- 50 visual aid
- 50 oral presentation
- 25 aesthetic considerations

SAMPLE "ALTERNATIVE ASSESSMENT PROJECTS"

SELF EVALUATION: ROMAN LITERARY FIGURES PROJECT

NOMEN_____ **DIES**_____

1. Please provide an honest assessment of the approximate amount of time (total hours) you spent working on the tasks for this project. Please itemize SPECIFIC tasks which you performed and how long you spent working on each task.

   Tasks include (but you may add others):
   Research
   writing an outline/rough draft
   writing the paper
   creating the visual aid
   presenting the material to the class
   Other tasks (please describe):

2. Please rate the quality and depth of your project according to the rubrics by placing an "X" in the box which best applies.

QUALITY OF PAPER, VISUAL AID, AND ORAL PRESENTATION	SUPERB= included exceptional level of detail; demonstrated considerable effort	ACCEPTABLE= included an adequate amount of detail; demonstrated solid effort	FAIR= included moderate amount of detail; demonstrated some effort	POOR= included some to little detail; represented a hurried project with minimal effort
text includes pertinent dates				
text includes important life cycle events (birth, death, marriage, children)				
text includes 5–8 other important facts (career, travel, personality, habits, contributions)				
visual aid relates to person				
visual aid contains 4–6 important facts				
speaking during oral report was clear, with adequate volume, and at an intelligible speed				
oral report provided information in an organized and understandable presentation				
Aesthetic quality of project (neatness, creativity, beauty)				

3. Please give yourself an overall grade: A   A-   B+   B   B-   C+   C   C-   D+   D   F

   Please explain why you gave yourself the grade you did in a **minimum** of 3–5 sentences below:

4. What aspects of the project should be altered so that it may be more understandable or work more smoothly in the future?

ROMAN LITERARY FIGURES GRADING RUBRIC   **NOMEN**_____

- **OPTIME =** demonstrated exceptional understanding / proficiency / effort / level of detail
- **BENE =** demonstrated acceptable understanding / proficiency / effort / level of detail
- **SATIS =** demonstrated moderate understanding / proficiency / effort / level of detail; could / should have done more work
- **NON SATIS =** demonstrated some or little understanding / proficiency / effort / level of detail; could / should have done considerably more work

	OPTIME	BENE	SATIS	NON SATIS
QUALITY OF INFORMATION				
important dates/events included (50 pts.) (life cycle, career, personality)	(50–44)	(43–37)	(36–30)	
additional appropriate (20 pts.) dates/events included	(20–17)	(16–13)	(12–8)	
accuracy of information (30 pts.)	(30–26)	(25–21)	(20–16)	
VISUAL AID				
relates to person (25 pts.)	(25–22)	(21–18)	(17–13)	
contains 4–6 impt. facts (25 pts.)	(25–22)	(21–18)	(17–13)	
ORAL PRESENTATION				
quality of voice (30 pts.) volume, clarity, speed	(30–26)	(25–21)	(20–16)	
organized presentation (20 pts.)	(20–17)	(16–12)	(12–8)	
AESTHETIC FEATURES				
neatness of presentation (5 pts.)	(5–4)	(3–2)	(1)	
creative presentation (5 pts.)	(5–4)	(3–2)	(1)	
spelling, punctuation, grammar (5 pts.)	(5–4)	(3–2)	(1)	
exceptional communication of ideas (5 pts.)	(5–4)	(3–2)	(1)	
exceptional detail of information (5 pts.)	(5–4)	(3–2)	(1)	

TOTAL POINTS (225 possible)
GRADE ADJUSTMENT (ON TIME?_____; # DAYS LATE_____)
COMMENTS:

SAMPLE "ALTERNATIVE ASSESSMENT PROJECTS"

PROJECT EVALUATION: ROMAN LITERARY FIGURES

1. Do you feel this project was more or less useful than individual readings, followed by a lecture and a test? Please make one-two comments on the positive/negative aspects of the project vs. lecture.

2. Did you spend more or less time preparing for the project than you would have for readings and a test? How did your use of preparation time differ?

3. Do your feel working with your classmates would have helped or hindered the project?

4. Tell me something new that you learned (about yourself or the material) as a result of this project, that you did not expect.

5. What other kinds of projects do you think would be fun and interesting to explore?

SAMPLE "ALTERNATIVE ASSESSMENT PROJECTS"

COMPARATIVE TIMELINE PROJECT NOMEN_____

Description: In this project, your task will be to create one timeline on which you chart the lives of two different people relative to each other. You and a partner will decide on the major events in each figure's life and plot them out with ample description.

Topics: Caesar vs. Catullus   Pompey vs. Horace   Octavian vs. Ovid

Sources:
- library and Internet research

Tasks:
- research the lives of the two people assigned
- produce a list of significant events from each figure's life along with the appropriate dates, including at a minimum those in the checklist below (if applicable):
  - ____ birth/death (manner, place)
  - ____ lineage/status (e.g. class, *novus homo*, etc.)
  - ____ spouse(s)/child(ren) (familial connections)
  - ____ military service (position, place)
  - ____ major battles and their outcomes
  - ____ military campaigns and/or appointments
  - ____ military triumphs/awards and/or failures/demotions
  - ____ political offices held
  - ____ political triumphs/awards and/or failures/demotions
  - ____ financial windfalls/disasters
  - ____ other jobs/positions held
  - ____ name changes
  - ____ periods of exile and circumstances of return (where appropriate)
  - ____ times that person's actions marked a change in precedence from earlier Roman history
- create a visual in which you plot these and other events chronologically along with the pertinent dates and an appropriate description of the event (especially its significance)
- present the timeline so that it easy for a viewer to compare the lives of each individual

Size: The timeline should be on sheets no smaller that 8.5" x 11," although you will probably find it easier to work on something bigger.

PROJECT DUE DATE: In class on_____. NO EXCEPTIONS. You and your partner will lose one full letter grade for each day the project is late.

NOTA BENE: You and your partner may not collaborate with another pair, or anyone else for that matter. Your final product must be the result of the work you two have done together.

Grading: 250 points total: 60 points per figure (thoroughness, depth) = 120
80 clarity and accuracy of information
50 neatness and creativity

SAMPLE "ALTERNATIVE ASSESSMENT PROJECTS"

SELF & PARTNER EVALUATION: COMPARATIVE TIMELINE PROJECT

NOMEN_____(required)_____ **DIES**_____

1. Please provide an honest assessment of the amount of time (total hours) **YOU** spent preparing your texts, discussions and/or visuals for this project. Please itemize SPECIFIC tasks which **YOU** performed to complete the project, and how long **YOU** spent working on each task.

   Tasks include (but you may add others):
   reading/taking notes during research phase:
   creating individual time lines for each historical figure:
   combining the time lines into one large composite time line:
   incorporating pictures or other visually pleasing features:
   computer time assembling the various pieces of the project:
   OTHER TASKS (PLEASE DESCRIBE):

2. NOW, please provide an honest assessment of the amount of time (total hours) **YOUR PARTNER** spent preparing your texts, discussions and/or visuals for this project. Please itemize SPECIFIC tasks which **YOUR PARTNER** performed to complete the project, and how long **YOUR PARTNER** spent working on each task.

   Tasks include (but you may add others):
   reading/taking notes during research phase:
   creating individual time lines for each historical figure:
   combining the time lines into one large composite time line:
   incorporating pictures or other visually pleasing features:
   computer time assembling the various pieces of the project:
   OTHER TASKS (PLEASE DESCRIBE):

3. Please rate the quality of your information according to the rubric by placing an "X" in the box which best applies.

QUALITY OF INFORMATION	SUPERB = included exceptional level of detail; emonstrated considerable effort	ACCEPTABLE = included an adequate amount of detail; demonstrated solid effort	FAIR = included moderate amount of detail; demonstrated some effort	POOR = included some to little detail; represented a hurried project with minimal effort
JULIUS CAESAR				
CATULLUS				
POMPEY				
HORACE				
OCTAVIAN				
OVID				
OTHER RELATED FIGURES (wives, children, influential friends, etc.)				

4. Overall assessment of historical information: SUPERB   ACCEPTABLE   FAIR   POOR

   Please explain your rating in 1–2 sentences.

5. Please rate the quality of your timeline's appearance according to the rubric by placing an "X" in the box which best applies.

QUALITY OF INFORMATION	SUPERB = included exceptional level of detail; demonstrated considerable effort	ACCEPTABLE = included an adequate amount of detail; demonstrated solid effort	FAIR= included moderate amount of detail; demonstrated some effort	POOR= included some to little detail; represented a hurried project with minimal effort
layout/format is easy to read and understand				
the data for each person was legible and easily connected to that person				
color was used to ornament the timeline				
illustration was used to ornament the timeline				
Latin phrases were incorporated in the data presented				

6. Overall assessment of timeline appearance: SUPERB   ACCEPTABLE   FAIR   POOR

   Please explain your rating in 1–2 sentences.

7. Please evaluate **YOUR** success in working as part of a group during the project. Describe SPECIFIC contributions which you made to help your group complete the project. If you feel you did not work as successfully as you might have wanted with your peers, describe areas in which you feel you could/should have contributed more fully. (NOTE: PLEASE BE HONEST. HAVING DIFFICULTIES AND LEARNING TO COPE WITH THEM IS ALSO PART OF THE LEARNING PROCESS.)

8. Please give yourself an overall grade: A   A-   B+   B   B-   C+   C   C-   D+   D   F

   Please explain why you gave yourself the grade you did in a **minimum** of 3–5 sentences below:

SAMPLE "ALTERNATIVE ASSESSMENT PROJECTS"

9. Please evaluate **YOUR PARTNER'S** success in working as part of a group during the project. Describe SPECIFIC contributions which he/she made to help your group complete the project. If you feel he/she did not work as successfully as you might have wanted with you, describe areas in which you feel he/she could/should have contributed more fully. (NOTE: PLEASE BE HONEST. HAVING DIFFICULTIES AND LEARNING TO COPE WITH THEM IS ALSO PART OF THE LEARNING PROCESS.)

10. Please give YOUR PARTNER an overall grade: A   A-   B+   B   B-   C+   C   C-   D+   D   F

    Please explain why you gave YOUR PARTNER the grade you did in a **minimum** of 3–5 sentences below:

11. What aspects of the project should be altered so that it may be more understandable or work more smoothly in the future?

COMPARATIVE TIMELINE GRADING RUBRIC NOMEN_____

OPTIME =	demonstrated exceptional understanding / proficiency / effort / level of detail
BENE =	demonstrated acceptable understanding / proficiency / effort / level of detail
SATIS =	demonstrated moderate understanding / proficiency / effort / level of detail; could / should have done more work
NON SATIS =	demonstrated some or little understanding / proficiency / effort / level of detail; could / should have done considerably more work

	OPTIME	BENE	SATIS	NON SATIS
QUALITY OF INFORMATION				
pertinent dates included (50 pts.) (cf. directions sheet)	(50–44)	(43–37)	(36–30)	
additional appropriate (20 pts.) dates/events included	(20–17)	(16–13)	(12–8)	
accuracy of information (50 pts.)	(50–44)	(43–37)	(36–30)	
CLARITY OF INFORMATION				
approp. depth of (30 pts.) articulation of events	(30–26)	(25–21)	(20–16)	
appropriately concise (30 pts.) presentation of information	(30–26)	(25–21)	(20–16)	
overall quality of writing and (20 pts.) organization of timeline	(20–17)	(16–12)	(12–8)	
AESTHETIC FEATURES				
neatness of presentation (10 pts.) (font / penmanship)	(10–9)	(8–7)	(6)	
creative presentation (10 pts.)	(10–9)	(8–7)	(6)	
spelling, punctuation, grammar (10 pts.)	(10–9)	(8–7)	(6)	
exceptional communication of ideas (10 pts.)	(10–9)	(8–7)	(6)	
exceptional detail of information (10 pts.)	(10–9)	(8–7)	(6)	

TOTAL POINTS
GRADE ADJUSTMENT (ON TIME?_____; # DAYS LATE_____)
COMMENTS:

PROJECT EVALUATION: COMPARATIVE TIMELINES

1. Do you feel this project was more or less useful than individual readings, followed by a lecture and a test? Please make one-two comments on the positive/negative aspects of the project vs. lecture.

2. Did you spend more or less time preparing for the project than you would have for readings and a test? How did your use of preparation time differ?

3. Do your feel working with your classmate helped or hindered the project? Did you enjoy the pair-partner experience?

4. Tell me something new that you learned (about yourself or the material) as a result of this project, that you did not expect.

5. What other kinds of projects do you think would be fun and interesting to explore?

PLACES AND PROVINCES RELATING TO ROME   NOMEN_____

Description: In this project, you and a partner will be doing research about a particular site. You will need to find out some specific items and decide with your partner what other information to include. As a team, you and your partner will share this information with your classmates in an oral presentation that will be accentuated by a visual aid.

Topics:
Verona, Italy	Philippi, Macedonia	Sicily
Bithynia	Venusia, Italy	Tomis (near Constanza, Rumania)
Alexandria, Egypt	Sulmo, Italy	Roman Forum (impt. bldgs.)
Athens, Greece	Actium, Greece	Rome (major districts)

Sources: library and Internet research

Tasks:
- research the site assigned
- create a written paper (3–5 pages) about that site.
- create a visual element appropriate to your topic
- infuse your paper and/or visual with memorable details
- present the details of your research orally in class, in an 8–10 minute presentation

Paper Parameters: In your site report, the following items MUST be addressed:
- location and founding / colonization of site
- special features of the site
- historical overview of the site through the centuries / millennia
- the excavation and/or restoration of the site in modern times

length: 3–5 pages of typed text about your topic, in Times New Roman, size 12 font
spacing: double-spaced, with one-inch, left-ruled margins
Title page and Bibliography

Visual:
- size = 8.5" x 11"
- must be appropriate for your topic (e.g. a layout of a battlefield, a labeled site plan/map)
- enough copies for each member of the class

Oral Presentation: Both team members must share speaking responsibilities, and the presentation must incorporate the use of the visual aid.

PROJECT DUE DATE: In class on_____. NO EXCEPTIONS. You and your partner will lose one full letter grade for each day the project is late.

NOTA BENE: You and your partner may not collaborate with another pair, or anyone else for that matter. Your final product must be the result of the work you two have done together.

Grading: 250 points total:
100 points paper
50 Visual Aid
75 Oral Presentation
25 Aesthetic Considerations

SAMPLE "ALTERNATIVE ASSESSMENT PROJECTS"

SELF & PARTNER EVALUATION: IMPORTANT SITES PROJECT

NOMEN_____(required)_____ DIES_____

1. Please provide an honest assessment of the amount of time (total hours) **YOU** spent preparing your texts, discussions and/or visuals for this project. Please comment upon SPECIFIC tasks which **YOU** performed to complete the project, and how long **YOU** spent working on each task:

    Tasks include (but you may add others):
    research
    writing an outline/rough draft
    writing the paper
    creating the visual aid
    presenting the material to the class
    other tasks (please describe):

2. NOW, please provide an honest assessment of the amount of time (total hours) **YOUR PARTNER** spent preparing your texts, discussions and/or visuals for this project. Please comment on SPECIFIC tasks which **YOUR PARTNER** performed to complete the project, and how long **YOUR PARTNER** spent working on each task.

    Tasks include (but you may add others):
    research
    writing an outline/rough draft
    writing the paper
    creating the visual aid
    presenting the material to the class
    other tasks (please describe):

3. Please rate the quality and depth of your project according to the rubrics by placing and "X" in the box which best applies.

QUALITY OF PAPER, VISUAL AID, AND ORAL PRESENTATION	SUPERB= included exceptional level of detail; demonstrated considerable effort	ACCEPTABLE = included an adequate amount of detail; demonstrated solid effort	FAIR = included moderate amount of detail; demonstrated some effort	POOR = included some to little detail; represented a hurried project with minimal effort
text includes required information				
text includes 5–8 other important facts of interest				
visual aid clearly relates to site				
speaking during oral report was clear, with adequate volume, and at an intelligible speed				
both team members contributed equally to oral presentation				
oral report provided information in an organized and understandable presentation				
oral presentation smoothly incorporated use of visual aid				
Aesthetic quality of project (neatness, creativity, beauty)				

4. Please give an overall assessment of your project and performance:

   SUPERB   ACCEPTABLE   FAIR   POOR

   Please explain your rating in 2–3 sentences.

5. Please evaluate **YOUR** success in working as part of a group during the project. Describe SPECIFIC contributions which you made to help your group complete the project. If you feel you did not work as successfully as you might have wanted with your peers, describe areas in which you feel you could/should have contributed more fully. (NOTE: PLEASE BE HONEST. HAVING DIFFICULTIES AND LEARNING TO COPE WITH THEM IS ALSO PART OF THE LEARNING PROCESS.)

6. Please give yourself an overall grade: A   A-   B+   B   B-   C+   C   C-   D+   D   F

   Please explain why you gave yourself the grade you did in a **minimum** of 3–5 sentences below:

SAMPLE "ALTERNATIVE ASSESSMENT PROJECTS"

7. Please evaluate **YOUR PARTNER'S** success in working as part of a group during the project. Describe SPECIFIC contributions which he/she made to help your group complete the project. If you feel he/she did not work as successfully as you might have wanted with you, describe areas in which you feel he/she could/should have contributed more fully. (NOTE: PLEASE BE HONEST. HAVING DIFFICULTIES AND LEARNING TO COPE WITH THEM IS ALSO PART OF THE LEARNING PROCESS.)

8. Please give YOUR PARTNER an overall grade: A   A-   B+   B   B-   C+   C   C-   D+   D   F

Please explain why you gave YOUR PARTNER the grade you did in a **minimum** of 3–5 sentences below.

SITE REPORT GRADING RUBRIC   NOMEN_____

OPTIME = demonstrated exceptional understanding / proficiency / effort / level of detail
BENE = demonstrated acceptable understanding / proficiency / effort / level of detail
SATIS = demonstrated moderate understanding / proficiency / effort / level of detail; could / should have done more work
NON SATIS = demonstrated some or little understanding / proficiency / effort / level of detail; could / should have done considerably more work

	OPTIME	BENE	SATIS	NON SATIS
QUALITY OF INFORMATION				
required information included (50 pts.)	(50–44)	(43–37)	(36–30)	
additional appropriate (20 pts.) information included	(20–17)	(16–13)	(12–8)	
accuracy of information (30 pts.)	(30–26)	(25–21)	(20–16)	
VISUAL AID				
relates to site (30 pts.)	(30–26)	(25–21)	(20–16)	
quality of visual aid (20 pts)	(20–17)	(16–12)	(12–8)	
ORAL PRESENTATION				
quality of voice (30 pts.) volume, clarity, speed	(30–26)	(25–21)	(20–16)	
organized presentation (20 pts.)	(20–17)	(16–12)	(12–8)	
utilized visual smoothly (15 pts.) in oral presentation	(20–17)	(16–12)	(12–8)	
both pair members contrib. (10 pts.) equally in oral presentation	(10–8)	(7–6)	(5–4)	
AESTHETIC FEATURES				
neatness of project (5 pts.)	(5–4)	(3–2)	(1)	
creative project (5 pts.)	(5–4)	(3–2)	(1)	
spelling, punctuation, grammar (5 pts.)	(5–4)	(3–2)	(1)	
exceptional communication of ideas (5 pts.)	(5–4)	(3–2)	(1)	
exceptional detail of information (5 pts.)	(5–4)	(3–2)	(1)	

TOTAL POINTS (225 possible)
GRADE ADJUSTMENT (ON TIME?_____ ; # DAYS LATE_____)
COMMENTS:

SAMPLE "ALTERNATIVE ASSESSMENT PROJECTS"

PROJECT EVALUATION: SITE REPORT

1. Do you feel this project was more or less useful than individual readings, followed by a lecture and a test? Please make one-two comments on the positive/negative aspects of the project vs. lecture.

2. Did you spend more or less time preparing for the project than you would have for readings and a test? How did your use of preparation time differ?

3. Do your feel working with your classmate helped or hindered the project? Did you enjoy the pair-partner experience?

4. Tell me something new that you learned (about yourself or the material) as a result of this project, that you did not expect.

5. What other kinds of projects do you think would be fun and interesting to explore?

SAMPLE "ALTERNATIVE ASSESSMENT PROJECTS"

FINAL PROJECT: CATULLUS, HORACE, OVID   NOMEN_____

Background: You will be asked to draw upon your knowledge of the poetry of Catullus, Horace and Ovid as read, discussed and reflected upon throughout this semester.

Objective: In this project, you will be focussing upon developing your creative sensitivity towards poetry. We have been reading and experiencing the poetry of three Roman lyric poets—Catullus, Horace and Ovid—and now it is your turn to explore your creative energies to interpret and produce poetry.

Parameters: The project contains three parts:
1. Illustrating selections from the works of Catullus, Horace and Ovid
2. Creating your own poetry (in English) "in the style" of these poets
3. Reciting 3 poems **in Latin** and **in meter;** reading 2 of your creations

The expectations in regard to each of these areas will be explained IN DETAIL below.

Requirements: There are five:
1. All students must participate.
2. Time allowed in class for planning and working on the project must be used for such. Failure to do so will be cause for reduction in your project points.
3. The final work which you submit must be neat, legible and appropriate in language and style. You may NOT turn in any final poem on lined, notebook-type paper. Your final work must be in booklet form, on 8 1/2 x 11" paper.
4. In order to complete the project on time, you will need to spend time at the computer lab **OUTSIDE** of class.
5. All students will need one computer disk (preferably two) in order to store the work for the project.

Grading: **THIS PROJECT SUBSTITUTES FOR THE FINAL EXAM.** It will be worth 20% of your semester grade (the amount usually allotted for a final exam).

300 possible points:
- 120 points   Illustrations
- 120 points   Original Poetry
- 60 points   Recitations

Points will be allotted based upon:
1. Fulfillment of the requirements above
2. Creativity
3. Involvement and Interest
4. Your booklet of poems
5. Your poetry presentation

For more details on grading, please refer to the self, peer, and teacher evaluation rubrics

DUE DATE: ALL BOOKLETS ARE DUE ON_____AT THE BEGINNING OF CLASS. YOU ARE REQUIRED TO HAND IN TWO COPIES OF YOUR BOOKLET. NO LATE WORK WILL BE ACCEPTED. FAILURE TO DO THIS WILL RESULT IN A GRADE OF ZERO. **NO EXCEPTIONS.**

SAMPLE "ALTERNATIVE ASSESSMENT PROJECTS"

Section 1: Illustrating selections from the works of Catullus, Horace and Ovid

Objective: In this section, you are trying to demonstrate your knowledge of a poem's theme and tone.

Requirements: 4 poems from Catullus; 4 poems from Horace; 4 poems from Ovid

Selecting: First, you must decide the themes upon which you would like to focus. For each poet, I would like you to use each theme only once. That is, you may not illustrate two of Catullus' love poems. You must choose ONE love poem and a poem with another type of theme. Because each poet may approach the same theme in a different fashion, however, you MAY choose to illustrate a love poem of Catullus, a love poem of Horace, and a love poem of Ovid.

Illustrating: Remember that for each poem, you are trying to create a mood as well as to convey a visual image of the theme. To convey mood, you may want to consider using a colored or textured background, or writing or typing your selection in a particular size or style of writing. For the visual image, you may want to draw or paint a picture, or superimpose the poem over an existing photograph, or create a "collage" from modern magazine photographs, or create some kind of computer-graphic image. The **Latin** text of each poem must be a part of each illustration.

Explaining: For each poem, on a separate sheet of paper, you must explain in a short paragraph why you expressed tone and theme as you chose to do, and the images and emotional responses you are trying to evoke from the reader/viewer.

Section 2: Creating your own poetry (in English) "in the style" of Catullus, Horace, and Ovid

Objective: In this section, you are trying to demonstrate your knowledge of theme, a poet's style, poetic devices, and tone.

Requirements: 3 "Catullan" poems; 2 "Horatian" poems; 1 "Ovidian" poem

Selecting: First, you must decide the themes upon which you would like to focus. For each poet, you may use each theme only once, and the themes selected must be **different** from the ones used in the illustration section.

Creating: Here, you have a number of options.
1. You can take a poem of Catullus (or Horace, or Ovid) and "translate" it as beautifully and as poetically as you can, just as in Catullus 87, where several modern poets gave their versions of Catullus' poem.
2. You can select a theme of a poet and then create a poem of your making on that theme in the style and tone of the author. For example, Catullus often ends a poem with the sudden shift of focus or biting remark in the last line, whereas Horace tends to modulate from one image to another as he moves through the stanzas.
3. Or, you could write a poem that copies the poetic devices of a poem but focuses upon a slightly different theme and/or tone. I'm thinking here of Catullus' "girl with the not pretty feet" poem, Horace's "now is the time for drinking" poem, or Ovid's "every lover is a soldier" poem.

Parameters:

1. If you choose to do a beautiful "translation," you may only do this for ONE poem. I want this project partially to be a self-exploration, and that will not happen if you do not step out on your own.

2. Your poems must be a minimum of four lines in length. I know that both Catullus and Horace admire conciseness, but you are bound to a minimum wordiness of four lines.

3. Somewhere in your poems, you must include the following poetic devices: chiasmus, synchesis, anaphora, litotes, alliteration, simile, metaphor, hyperbole, synecdoche, metonymy, juxtaposition, and oxymoron. Here, you are required to use 3 separate devices per poem as a minimum. You may reuse a device in the same poem (but then it doesn't "count") and you may also use the same device in another poem. If you're truly laboring with a poetic device, see me.

4. I expect three drafts of each creation to be handed in (though only the final version will appear in your booklet). With these poems, I am looking for quality, not quantity. As you compose your poems, you may want to consider writing drafts in the following manner: Draft 1 = ideas; Draft 2 = add poetic devices; Final version = increase the sophistication of your language. If you would like to "draft" in other ways, see me.

5. I prefer that the final version of your poems be submitted in typed form (though you can print them out in a beautiful font in you so choose). If you hand-write your final version, it must be neat and easily readable. If you are not sure that your work can be read, SHOW IT TO ME IN ADVANCE. Any work that I cannot read easily will receive a zero.

6. You do not HAVE to create poetry in the meters of the poets—or in ANY meter for that matter—but you can try to do so if you would like.

7. Similarly, your poetry does not have to rhyme, though it of course MAY rhyme if you would like to create it in this way.

8. You do not have to compose poetry in Latin, but if you would like to attempt this, I would be more than happy to help you with this endeavor.

Section 3: Recitations

Part I. Reciting three poems **in Latin** and **in meter**

Objective: In this part of Section 3, you are demonstrating your understanding of the pronunciation of Latin and of the rhythm of Latin poetry. Through recitation, you can also display your knowledge of mood and the meaning of the Latin words.

Requirements: Catullus 13; Horace I.38; Ovid *Amores* III.15

SAMPLE "ALTERNATIVE ASSESSMENT PROJECTS"

Practice:
1. You do not have to memorize your poem.
2. Scan the poems in advance and have your scansion checked by your teacher so that you know you have no mistakes.
3. Refer back to your translation and discussion questions for each poem. Knowing the literal meaning and inner workings of the poem will help you demonstrate your interpretation of the poem while you recite. Use your knowledge of the poem to emphasize certain words appropriately, to create pauses in your reading, perhaps even to recite in a certain tone of voice.
4. Practice saying the poem ALOUD several times, concentrating upon effective pauses and vocal intonation to convey meaning. Your primary criteria, however, should be to speak with proper pronunciation and metrical accuracy.
5. Be warned about speaking too quickly. Practice your poem in a normal tone of voice and SLOWLY. When you recite before your peers, you will be nervous, and as a result, you will tend to speak too quickly.

Performance:
1. I plan to videotape your recitations, so be prepared. If you are truly concerned about losing your composure while you speak before the class, you may record your recitation on an audio tape in advance and hand it in with your project. You still must read publicly, but this will allow me to hear you at your best, should your public declamation be less than you hoped.
2. If you wish, you may dress in costume (modern dress) to help create mood and enhance the drama of your performance. (NOT REQUIRED)
3. The poems you recite must also be included in your booklet. Type or NEATLY hand-write each poem, scan it, and place them as the final poems in your booklet.

Part II. Reading two of your own poems

Objective: In this part of Section 3, you are sharing a portion of your creative output with your peers. This exercise will enable you and them to appreciate the varying ways the poetry of Catullus, Horace and Ovid can affect and inspire different individuals.

Practice: As with the Latin poems, please practice your poems before you recite them (see #4 and 5 above). Practicing will allow for a smoother reading and will help you to convey your own themes and ideas more effectively.

Performance: Before you begin the reading of each of your poems, please state the Latin poet and theme (or poem) from which you drew inspiration for your own creation.

ABSENCE: Your recitation is part of your final project. Should you be absent on the day of your recitation, <u>you must be prepared to recite</u> **ON THE DAY YOU RETURN**. If your absence is unexcused for the day you recite, you will receive a <u>**zero**</u> for that portion of your project.

POETRY PROJECT TEACHER-STUDENT CONFERENCE INFORMATION

STUDENT _____

POEMS SELECTED	CATULLUS	HORACE	OVID
ILLUSTRATIONS	1.	1.	1.
	2.	2.	2.
	3.	3.	3.
	4.	4.	4.
ORIGINAL POETRY	1.	1.	1.
	2.	2.	
	3.		
RECITATIONS / SCANNING			

ORIGINAL POETRY DISCUSSION	DRAFT 1	DRAFT 2	DRAFT 3
CATULLUS			
HORACE			
OVID			

SAMPLE "ALTERNATIVE ASSESSMENT PROJECTS"

Name of Person Evaluating:_____   Name of Person Reciting:_____

DIRECTIONS: CIRCLE THE POEM BEING RECITED AND THE APPROPRIATE STATEMENTS THAT APPLY.

	CATULLUS 13	**HORACE I.38**	**OVID** *AMORES* **III.15**	
1. **Pronunciation of words:**	all words pronounced correctly	a few words mispronounced	several words mispronounced	many words mispronounced
2. **Smoothness of fluid Pronunciation:**	a few stumbles	several stumbles	very disconnected speaking	
3. **Metricality:**	meter too dominant	meter conveyed but not too strongly	poem not delivered with any real sense of rhythm/meter	
4. **Volume of Voice:**	too loud	appropriate	somewhat hard to hear	difficult to hear (too soft)
5. **Speed of Voice:**	too quick	a little too fast	appropriate	a little too slow	unnaturally slow
6. **Tone of Voice:**	very dramatic	conveyed some emotion	words spoken but with little emotion	

Please describe the feelings or emotions you feel the speaker expressed:

_____

7. **Physical presence:**	very stiff; unnatural	formal; dignified	relaxed; at ease	poor posture; overly casual

Please describe any body postures or gestures the speaker used to good effect.

_____

8. Please describe any ideas present in the poem that you feel the speaker conveyed effectively:

_____

9. Costume: (NOT REQUIRED) Describe how the speaker's costume (if any) added to his/her performance:

_____

10. Please add any other comments about the speaker's performance that you feel need mentioning.

_____

OVERALL RATING: EXCELLENT   VERY GOOD   GOOD   ACCEPTABLE   NOT ACCEPTABLE

SELF EVALUATION: POETRY PROJECT

NOMEN_____ **DIES**_____

1. Please provide an honest assessment of the approximate amount of time (total hours) you spent working on the tasks for this project. Please itemize SPECIFIC tasks which you performed and how long you spent working on each task.

   Tasks include (but you may add others):
   - selecting poems
   - creating illustrations
   - creating original poetry
   - scanning recitation poems
   - practicing for recitation

2. Please discuss the tasks. Which were more "fun," and why? Which were more challenging, and why?

3. Please rate the quality and depth of your project according to the rubrics by placing and "X" in the box which best applies.

QUALITY OF ILLUSTRATIONS, ORIGINAL POETRY, AND RECITATION	SUPERB = included exceptional level of detail; demonstrated considerable effort	ACCEPTABLE = included an adequate amount of detail; demonstrated solid effort	FAIR = included moderate amount of detail; demonstrated some effort	POOR = included some to little detail; represented a hurried project with minimal effort
Catullus illustrations				
Horace illustrations				
Ovid illustrations				
Catullan creations				
Horatian creations				
Ovidian creation				
poetic device usage				
voice during recitation was clear, with adequate volume, and at an intelligible speed				
ability to pronounce Latin words				
ability to recite Latin poetry in meter				
Aesthetic quality of project (neatness, creativity, beauty)				

4. Please tell me something that you learned (about yourself or the material) as a result of this project, that you did not expect.

5. Please give yourself an overall grade: A   A-   B+   B   B-   C+   C   C-   D+   D   F

   Please explain why you gave yourself the grade you did in a **minimum** of 3–5 sentences below:

6. What aspects of the project should be altered so that it may be more understandable or work more smoothly in the future?

FINAL POETRY PROJECT GRADING RUBRIC

NOMEN_____

OPTIME =	demonstrated exceptional understanding / proficiency / effort / level of detail	
BENE =	demonstrated acceptable understanding / proficiency / effort / level of detail	
SATIS =	demonstrated moderate understanding / proficiency / effort / level of detail; could / should have done more work	
NON SATIS =	demonstrated some or little understanding / proficiency / effort / level of detail; could / should have done considerably more work	

	OPTIME	**BENE**	**SATIS**	**NON SATIS**
ILLUSTRATIONS (120 pts.)				
4 Catullus illustrations (12 pts.)	(12–10)	(9–7)	(6–4)	
4 Horace illustrations (12 pts.)	(12–10)	(9–7)	(6–4)	
4 Ovid illustrations (12 pts.)	(12–10)	(9–7)	(6–4)	
1 explanation (in English) per illustration (12 pts).	(12–10)	(9–7)	(6–4)	
Complete Latin text present for each poem (12 pts.)	(12–10)	(9–7)	(6–4)	
Mood of each poem conveyed (24 pts.)	(24–20)	(19–15)	(14–10)	
Relevance of each illustration (24 pts.)	(24–20)	(19–15)	(14–10)	
Evidence of careful time spent in completion of each illustration (12 pts.)	(12–10)	(9–7)	(6–4)	
Latin caption for each illustration (optional)	(yes)	(no)		

Teacher comments:

SAMPLE "ALTERNATIVE ASSESSMENT PROJECTS"

	OPTIME	BENE	SATIS	NON SATIS
ORIGINAL POETRY (120 pts.)				
3 Catullus creations (6 pts.)	(6–5)	(4–3)	(2–1)	
2 Horace creations (4 pts.)	(4)	(3–2)	(1)	
1 Ovid creation (2 pts.)	(2)			
3 poetic devices per poem (18 pts.)	(18–17)	(16–15)	(14–12)	
authenticity of Catullan style (24 pts.)	(24–20)	(19–15)	(14–10)	
authenticity of Horatian style (24 pts.)	(24–20)	(19–15)	(14–10)	
authenticity of Ovidian style (24 pts.)	(24–20)	(19–15)	(14–10)	
aesthetics of presentation (6 pts.)	(6–5)	(4–3)	(2–1)	
evidence of careful time spent in creation of poems (6 pts.)	(6–5)	(4–3)	(2–1)	
2 rough drafts submitted for each creation (6 pts.)	(yes)	(no)		
not more than 1 beautiful translation	(yes)	(no)		
length restrictions observed (4-line minimum/poem)	(yes)	(no)		
each required poetic device used	(yes)	(no)		

    chiasmus   synchesis   anaphora   litotes   alliteration   simile
    metaphor   hyperbole   synecdoche   metonymy   juxtaposition   oxymoron

OPTIONAL ITEMS

meter	(yes)	(no)		
rhyme	(yes)	(no)		
in Latin	(yes)	(no)		
add'l other poetic devices	(yes)	(no)		

Teacher comments:

SAMPLE "ALTERNATIVE ASSESSMENT PROJECTS"

	OPTIME	BENE	SATIS	NON SATIS
RECITATIONS (60 pts.)				
Latin recitation poems included (6 pts.) as final pages of booklet	(6–5)	(4–3)	(2–1)	
poems scanned correctly (6 pts.)	(6–5)	(4–3)	(2–1)	
pronunciation of Latin words (6 pts.)	(6–5)	(4–3)	(2–1)	
smoothness/fluency of recitation (6 pts.)	(6–5)	(4–3)	(2–1)	
metricality (6 pts.)	(6–5)	(4–3)	(2–1)	
volume of voice (6 pts.)	(6–5)	(4–3)	(2–1)	
speed of voice (6 pts.)	(6–5)	(4–3)	(2–1)	
tone of voice (6 pts.)	(6–5)	(4–3)	(2–1)	
physical presence while speaking (6 pts.)	(6–5)	(4–3)	(2–1)	
evidence of thoughtful preparation (6 pts.)	(6–5)	(4–3)	(2–1)	
props/costume (optional)	(yes)	(no)		

Teacher comments:

ILLUSTRATIONS GRADE   (OUT OF 120)   _____

ORIGINAL POETRY GRADE   (OUT OF 120)   _____

RECITATION GRADE   (OUT OF 60)   _____

OVERALL PROJECT GRADE   (OUT OF 300)   _____

BIBLIOGRAPHY

CATULLUS

J. Ferguson, *Catullus*. Lawrence, KS, 1985.

P. Y. Forsyth, *Catullus. A Teaching Text*. Lanham, MD, 1986.

D. H. Garrison, *The Student's Catullus*. Norman, OK, 1995.

R. O. A. M. Lyne, *Selections from Catullus: Handbook*. Cambridge, 1975.

K. Quinn, *Catullus. The Poems*. London, 1973.

S. G. P. Small, *Catullus. A Reader's Guide to the Poems*. Lanham, MD, 1983.

HORACE

R. Ancona, *Horace. Selected* Odes *and* Satire I. 9. Wauconda, 1999.

H. V. Bender, *A Horace Reader for Advanced Placement*. Newburyport, MA, 1998.

D. H. Garrison, *Horace.* Epodes *and* Odes. *A New Annotated Latin Edition*. Norman, OK, 1991.

K. Quinn, *Horace. The* Odes. London, 1980.

OVID

C. A. Jestin and P. B. Katz, *Ovid.* Amores, Metamorphoses. *Selections*. Wauconda, 2000.

GENERAL

American Classical League, *Standards for Classical Language Learning*. Oxford, OH, 1997.

M. Balme and J. Morwood, *Oxford Latin Course. Part III*. Oxford, 1995.

R. Maltby, *Latin Love Elegy*. Wauconda, 1985.

C. A. Murphy, D. G. Thiem, and R. T. Moore, *Embers of the Ancient Flame. Latin Love Poetry. Selections from Catullus, Horace and Ovid*. Wauconda, 2001.

P. Rutherford, *Instructions for All Students*. Alexandria, VA, 1998.

LEGAMUS TRANSITIONAL READERS

The *LEGAMUS Transitional Readers* are innovative texts that form a bridge between the initial study of Latin via basal textbooks and the reading of authentic author texts. This series of texts is being developed by a special committee of high school and college teachers to facilitate this challenging transition.

VERGIL: A LEGAMUS Transitional Reader

Thomas J. Sienkewicz and LeaAnn A. Osburn

This reader contains selections (about 200 lines) from Vergil's *Aeneid*, Books I, II, and IV, designed for students moving from elementary or intermediate Latin into reading the authentic Latin of Vergil. Passages are accompanied by pre-reading materials, grammatical exercises, complete vocabulary, notes designed for reading comprehension, and other reading aids. Introductory materials and illustrations are included.

xxvi + 136 pp. (2004) 8 ½" x 11" Paperback, ISBN 978-0-86516-578-6

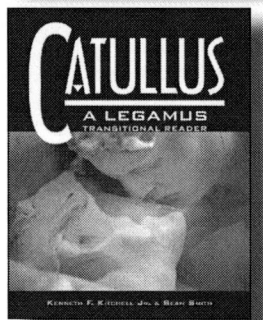

CATULLUS: A LEGAMUS Transitional Reader

Kenneth F. Kitchell Jr. and Sean Smith

This reader introduces students to eighteen Catullus poems. Introductory materials include an overview of the life and work of Catullus, bibliography, and description of Catullan meters. Appendices on grammar and figures of speech, and a pull-out vocabulary complete the book's innovative features. After finishing *Catullus: A LEGAMUS Transitional Reader*, students will be prepared to undertake a more complete study of Catullus as an AP* or college level course.

xxx + 162 pp. (2006) 8 ½" x 11" Paperback, ISBN 978-0-86516-634-9

OVID: A LEGAMUS Transitional Reader

Caroline Perkins and Denise Davis-Henry

This reader contains lines of Latin selections from Ovid poems, designed for students moving from elementary or intermediate Latin into reading the authentic Latin of Ovid. Introductory materials include an overview of the life and work of Ovid, bibliography, and description of Ovidian meters.

xxvi + 126 pp. (2007) 8 ½" x 11" Paperback, ISBN 978-0-86516-604-2

FORTHCOMING TO SERIES

CICERO: A LEGAMUS Transitional Reader
Judith Sebesta and Mark Haynes
(Forthcoming) Paperback, ISBN 978-0-86516-656-1

HORACE: A LEGAMUS Transitional Reader
Ronnie Ancona and David J. Murphy
(Forthcoming) Paperback, ISBN TBA

*AP is a registered trademark of the College Entrance Examination Board, which was not involved in the production of, and does not endorse, this product.

BOLCHAZY-CARDUCCI PUBLISHERS, INC.
www.BOLCHAZY.com